WRITER'S GUIDE

Psychology

ND

ISTRALE

with TOBY FULWILER

ARTHUR W. BIDDLE, *General Editor*

all of University of Vermont

D. C. HEATH AND COMPANY

Lexington, Massachusetts *Toronto*

Published simultaneously in Canada.

Printed in the United States of America.

International Standard Book Number: 0-669-12004-9

Library of Congress Catalog Card Number: 86-82608

Dedication

We dedicate this book to our spouses — David and Jennifer — who provided the support, the encouragement, and the child care necessary for us to complete this project.

Preface

One of the best ways to learn psychology is by writing it — that's the guiding principle behind this book. *Writer's Guide: Psychology* applies current writing theory and pedagogy to the specific needs of psychology. As a result, this book is a guide for psychology students at every level — from introductory coursework to advanced seminars.

TO THE STUDENT

This book is designed to help you write in psychology. Your professor may not ask you to read every chapter in this book, and it is likely that you will produce only a few of the writing assignments in any one course. But whether this is your first psychology course or your last, *Writer's Guide* offers you practical assistance and encouragement in handling the most important as well as the most typical writing tasks in the discipline. *Writer's Guide* will teach you, for example, how to compose a literature review by a step-by-step approach, from the prewriting stages of finding a topic and narrowing it down, to the actual writing of a clear and concise paper. Best of all, since we emphasize a process approach to writing, *Writer's Guide* will give you a definite alternative to last-minute papers and reports. Writing should be an important part of any course, even if you aren't required to complete formal papers. With this in mind, *Writer's Guide* describes how to use writing in journals to stimulate your own thinking. It also explains how to write better exams.

TO THE INSTRUCTOR

Written by a psychologist and a writing specialist, *Writer's Guide: Psychology* applies current and innovative aspects of composition theory to content-based writing in psychology. Since the text graduates in difficulty, it contains chapters appropriate for students at every level of study. Moving from the introductory prewriting and composing strategies in the first chapters, to generating summaries and abstracts and structuring examination answers, to writing literature reviews, research proposals, and finally research reports, this book thoroughly examines the major types of writing assigned in psychology. Basic tools of research and writing are also explained: procedures for library research, documentation style, grammatical usage, and punctuation. Therefore, *Writer's Guide* is designed as a supplementary text and reference manual for any and every psychology course or as a core text for a writing-across-the-curriculum program.

Each chapter of *Writer's Guide* is self-instructional. Although the value of many assignments would be enhanced by class discussion, students can use this book independently. In fact, the book was designed to help you, the instructor, give assignments without having to spend hours explaining the procedures for completing those tasks. Each chapter is presented in steps, each step culminates in a writing assignment, and each assignment leads to the next, until the student has a finished product. You can assign a chapter as a means of assigning a paper. Moreover, using this book will improve your students' understanding of psychology as it increases their writing ability.

Acknowledgements

The authors express their appreciation to many people for their assistance in preparing this book. Our greatest debt is owed to our students. A graduate seminar in Writing in Psychology sparked many of the ideas that went into *Writer's Guide*. In this and other psychology courses as well as writing classes, students field-tested most of the material and gave very practical advice for improvements. The majority of writing samples in this book came out of those classes. We're grateful to the authors for permission to use their work.

We also had great assistance from friends and colleagues. In particular, Bill Biddle, the *Writer's Guide* general editor, offered invaluable feedback and support. Faculty and graduate students in the Psychology Department at the University of Vermont contributed insights and experience which shaped many of the chapters of this book; we are particularly grateful to Larry Gordon, Dave Howell, Mark Bouton, and Patty Sunderland for their contributions. Other colleagues have been especially supportive: Virginia Clark, Mary Jane Dickerson, Toby Fulwiler, Ken Holland, and Hank Steffens from the University of Vermont, and Dan Bean from St. Michael's College. We also wish to thank Christine Starnes and the writing-across-the-curriculum faculty at John Abbott College, Montreal, Quebec, who gave us a critical forum for presenting material in this book. At D. C. Heath we are indebted especially to the patient encouragement of Holt Johnson and Paul Smith, as well as to their production editor, Laurie Johnson, and the outside reviewers who supplied us with thoughtful advice throughout the writing of this manuscript: Ellen Strensky, UCLA; Janet Carr, Northeastern University; Michael Moran, Clemson University; and Scott Rice, San Jose State University.

Lynne A. Bond
Anthony S. Magistrale
June, 1986
Burlington, Vermont

Contents

[1] *Writing in Psychology*

WHY WRITE?

That's a very good question. You enrolled in a psychology course, not a writing workshop. Now you find that you're expected to produce a lot of writing. Why?

Writing will help you develop your thinking skills. People all over the world seem to go through similar stages of cognitive development. As young children, they think on very concrete levels — in terms of actions and objects they have experienced. As they mature, they become more able to think in the abstract — in terms of possibilities rather than concrete reality. But some people develop these abstract thinking skills more than others. Cross-cultural research (e.g., Cole, 1978; Greenfield & Bruner, 1966) suggests that writing actually helps us develop these most sophisticated thinking skills. Writing forces us to separate our thinking from concrete events; we manipulate symbols (words) rather than objects themselves. This helps us to think in terms of new possibilities rather than be limited to our own experiences.

Writing will help you learn psychology. You've probably discovered the principle behind this fact already, maybe through sports or a job, perhaps by working on a lab experiment. We learn best not as passive recipients of lectures and textbooks, but as active participants, making meaning for ourselves. Writing is one of the best ways to get involved in your own education. That's what this book is all about — writing to learn. Your personal involvement through writing will lead you to a fuller understanding of psychology.

Writing helps you store your thoughts. The human mind is a marvel unmatched by the most advanced computer. Still, most of us don't seem to command the kind of memory we'd like or need. Written language provides a backup for your memory and access to limitless information.

Writing organizes your thoughts. When you have a lot to accomplish, you make a list of "things to do." When you prepare a speech or a class presentation, you jot down main ideas, then reassemble them into some sort of meaningful pattern. Combining invisible thoughts with the physical activity of forming words on paper helps you to discover and organize what you're thinking. Committing your thinking to the page focuses those thoughts.

Writing helps you to find the gaps in your logic or understanding. Let's say you read a chapter in your textbook or listen to a lecture on human aggression. Writing what you comprehend helps you to review, organize, and remember the material. But as you write, you also discover what is difficult for you to express — the concepts or theories that you don't understand thoroughly. By putting your questions on paper, by writing about your confusion, you begin to see just where your difficulty lies — what's missing in your logic, or where your knowledge is lacking. Often, you can write your way to understanding. Even if you can't, you'll know which issues to rethink, which parts of the chapter to reread, or which notes to review.

Writing reveals your attitude toward a subject. Perhaps you're asked to read two articles about the wisdom of using drugs to control hyperactive behavior. As you study the first essay, you find the arguments in favor of drug use are persuasive. Then you read the second, opposing, piece, and that sounds convincing too. It's sometimes hard to figure out just what you really think. What can you do? Listing the pros and cons of each perspective helps you see the strengths and weaknesses of both sides. Writing can help you discover how you feel about the issue. Then you're on the way to defining your own position.

Writing helps you synthesize large amounts of information. As you write down information and ideas, you often discover interrelationships in the content. You find yourself using similar words or related examples; you suddenly arrive at new connections within the material. Writing allows you to discover new ways of solving a problem. It also reveals new questions which are worth pursuing.

Writing is communication. Michael Foucault, the French philosopher and social scientist, observed that language functions to "tame the wild profusion of existing things" (1966/1970, p. 15). Writing brings order to the stream of conflicting information that our brain continually receives from our senses. Through the vehicle of writing, we conceptualize, categorize, and organize sensory perceptions into comprehensible patterns.

Words are the symbols of ideas and emotions. They are one way of measuring what we share with other people. Used correctly, they convey thoughts, arouse emotions, motivate action. As Foucault and others have pointed out, language can be the foundation and essence of a civilization, but writing is the medium that defines, for the most part, the boundaries of our communication.

YOU AND THE WRITING PROCESS

Your professor assigns a paper, due at the end of the semester. You're not told much more about it — you may get a list of acceptable topics or learn how many pages to write. Then, despite your best intentions, you wait until a few days before the due date to get started. If this has never happened to you, you're unusual.

Obviously, there are better ways of doing things. Whether you need to write a term paper, a seminar presentation, or a book review — virtually any communication — the most effective means is the **process approach.** Using this method of composition, you work your way through three broad stages: **prewriting, drafting,** and **revising.** Most experienced writers work this way. And writers-in-training have been found to make the greatest improvement when they take this approach.

Prewriting

All the preparations the writer makes before starting to draft — that's what we mean by prewriting. Among these preparations are finding a topic, limiting that topic to a manageable size, defining the purpose of the writing, assessing the audience, choosing a point of view, researching or interviewing, and taking notes. This prewriting stage of the process is much more crucial than many realize. You'll take the first steps in the next two sections, The Writer's Decisions and Techniques for Getting Started, and in Chapter 2, Using a Journal. In subsequent chapters, we'll discuss prewriting tasks that are specific to individual types of writing assignments.

Drafting

The second stage of the composing process, drafting, is what most people have in mind when they think of writing. Drafting is getting the words down on paper, which is much easier when you use the process approach.

Revising

Revising, the third stage, involves much more than most writers-in-training suspect. Example: This chapter is now in its fifth draft. In other words, it has been revised four times. That's why professional writers have such big wastebaskets — they keep working on a piece until it feels right. If you were to look up the word *revise* in the dictionary, you would find that it comes from the Latin *revidere* — to see again. True revision means just that, seeing again, looking once more at a draft with a willingness to consider changes, often big changes. You'll learn more about making these changes as you proceed through this book. Then, after you've revised your way to a good piece of work, refer to Chapter 9, Documentation Style Sheet; Chapter 10, A Concise Guide to Usage; and Chapter 11, Make Punctuation Work for You, for help with editing. Editing and proofreading are the final steps before submitting your work to the reader or editor.

THE WRITER'S DECISIONS

During the prewriting phase, before beginning to draft, the writer confronts several questions: Why am I writing this? Who's going to read it? What will they be expecting? How should my voice sound? Consciously or not, writers must answer these questions each time they sit down to write. Whether you are researching a term paper for your Experimental Psychology course, applying to graduate school, or writing a textbook in physiological psychology, the questions are the same. Only the answers are different.

What is this piece about?
Your answer to this question establishes the **subject,** the true topic of this piece of writing.

Why am I writing this? What do I want this to accomplish?
In answering these questions you decide about purpose. **Purpose** is your intent, the reason that moves you to write and the desired result of that effort.

Whom am I writing this for?
The answer to this question identifies your audience. **Audience** is the reader or readers you are addressing.

Who am I as I write this?
The answer to this question defines your voice. **Voice** is the character, personality, and attitude you project toward your subject, purpose, and audience.

Subject, purpose, audience, and voice are controls in any job of writing. Once you make decisions or accept conditions concerning them, you establish certain boundaries. Style, tone, readability, even organization and use of examples are all governed by these initial choices.

Figure 1.1 on p. 6 attempts to show how the four decisions relate to each other. At the center is the **subject,** the focus of any piece of writing. But often equally important and influential are the **purpose, audience,** and **voice.** Although you can characterize each of these elements independently, you'll find that each affects the others. And while the subject is typically the writer's first decision, in practice, this decision sequence may vary.

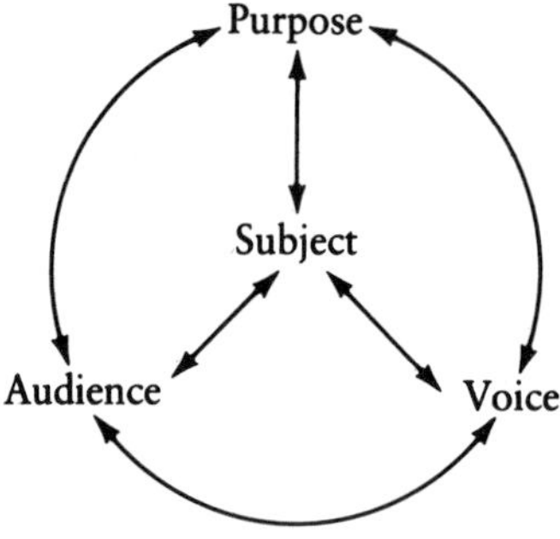

Figure 1.1 *The writer's decisions*

Decision 1: The Subject

Finding something to write about is often the hardest of the pre-writing tasks for writers-in-training. In the "real world," of course, you would write only when you felt it would be useful to you or others. In college courses, however, you are often told to write, whether you want to or not. That's because your instructors view the writing process as a way to learn and to express understanding. One objective in most psychology courses is to learn to perceive the world as a psychologist. That means asking the questions, mastering the information, and formulating the problems in the same ways that a psychologist does.

One of the best solutions to the problem of finding a **subject** is to anticipate it. Keeping a psychology journal will provide you with dozens of ideas for writing. In Chapter 2, Using a Journal, you'll learn about how this is done.

Whatever subject you choose should meet the following specifications:

1. It should fit the assignment. Does the subject fall into the scope of the course? A paper on techniques of art therapy, for instance, is inappropriate for a course in social psychology. Does the paper come within the limits established by the assignment? An account of Freud's theory of the subconscious would not fit the assignment to "write a paper about a *new* perspective on factors affecting human behavior."

2. It should be of interest to you. This is an obvious criterion, but one that students often overlook. If you are to spend thirty or forty hours researching and writing a paper, you should feel some intellectual excitement about the subject. Of course, you might discover a new interest as you read about a topic you thought dull at first. But begin with a question you genuinely want to answer.

3. It should be limited to allow adequate depth and breadth of coverage. If the assignment calls for a six- to eight-page paper, a topic like "the development of psychoses" is doomed to failure. Simply identifying the various types of psychoses would require more than six to eight pages; therefore, your paper would inevitably be superficial. However, limiting that broad topic could lead to some very workable subjects: behavioral precursors of manic-depressive disorder, for example, or proposed chemical bases of schizophrenia.

Chapter 5, The Literature Review, and Chapter 6, The Research Proposal, will discuss techniques for finding paper topics which meet these three criteria.

> WRITING 1.1: FINDING A SUBJECT. Based upon the subject criteria described above, write a list of five topics, suitable for a six- to eight-page paper, concerning the subject of human aggression or another topic relevant to your course.

Decision 2: Purpose

The purpose of a piece of writing can be complex, for it includes both the reason that moves you to write and the desired outcome. If you're writing a book review because your professor told you to, the professor's requirement provides one dimension of purpose. That requirement is not sufficient purpose to generate an effective review, however. You need to question yourself more closely: Why was I asked to write this? What does a book review do? You may then decide that you were asked to do the review to get you to read the book, think about it, and analyze its themes in relation to the course.

Very likely most of the psychology writing you'll do will be either to explain or to persuade. A further classification of kinds of explanation — exposition, as it is often called — follows. (Chapter 4 will discuss each of these in greater detail).

- **Definition:** Used to answer the question, "What is it?" of your subject. Example: "What is a stereotype?"
- **Classification:** Used to answer the question, "What is the pattern?" of your subject. Example: "What are the various forms of neuroses?"
- **Comparison and Contrast:** Used to answer the question, "What is it like or unlike?" of your subject. Example: "What are the similarities and differences between escape and avoidance conditioning?"
- **Analysis:** Used to answer the question, "What are the relationships among the parts?" of your subject. Example: "What are the major features of the central nervous system?"

  And, if your purpose combines explanation and persuasion:
- **Argumentation:** Used to answer the question, "Can you prove it?" of your subject. Example: "Should children be permitted to watch as much television as they wish?"

WRITING 1.2: DEFINING PURPOSE. Begin with a broad subject such as operant conditioning, schizophrenia, or conformity. Then ask of that subject each of the questions listed above, for instance, "What is operant conditioning? What are the various forms of operant conditioning?" and so on. Write your responses. The purpose of this exercise is to learn how these questions can help you sharpen a subject and focus your writing.

Decision 3: Audience

When you speak, you always speak to someone: your **audience.** It may be just one person, a group of friends, or your entire class. You know who the listener is and can see and hear reactions; you can tailor your talk to that audience, even modify it according to the responses you get. When you write, however, your audience is unseen and perhaps even unknown. If your audience doesn't understand something you write, it cannot ask you to explain yourself. These differences between the speaker/listener relationship and the writer/reader relationship point to the importance of the writer's decisions about audience.

Defining your audience can have an important influence on your writing. Let's take an example: You are asked to write an essay which explains factors affecting physical attractiveness. But who is your audience? Who will be reading the essay? Will it be students in an Introductory Psychology class, students in an Advanced Social Psychology class, fashion designers, or high school students? Although the subject seems to remain the same (factors affecting physical attractiveness), the requirements of these audiences are different. You can write much more effectively if you can precisely define your audience.

What exactly does the writer need to know about the audience for a particular piece of writing? Although the answers to that question depend partly on the **purpose** of the writing, here are some useful questions to ask:

What does the audience already know about the subject?

What are its expectations likely to be? its attitudes?

What is the age of the audience? the job? income?

What is the audience's educational level?

What other special needs of this audience should you take into account?

By asking these questions about the audience you get a much better idea of how to direct that writing.

How should you go about defining audience for your course assignments? First, ask your professor whether there is a particular audience you should have in mind. If not, here are your options:

1. You can write for the professor, the most common way of defining the audience of a student paper. The problem with addressing this audience is often in defining exactly who your professor is and what his or her expectations are.

2. You can write for the entire class, students and professor. If you do, you're likely to be less pompous and more direct than you would be addressing the professor alone. How else might your work differ?

3. You can write for yourself, as you might in a journal (see Chapter 2). Practically every writer-in-training would benefit from producing more of this prose.

4. You can write for a specified audience, such as parents, families of psychiatric clients, or professionals in another field, e.g., doctors or politicians.

5. You can write for scholars in the field, as if you were composing an article for a professional journal. The best way to get a sense of this audience's expectations is to read several articles in psychology journals.

> WRITING 1.3: DEFINING AUDIENCE. Choose a topic that you are currently studying, like the measurement of intelligence or the development of language skills. Write an explanation of the ways that you might adapt your treatment of that topic for each of the five audiences listed above. Be specific about your audiences' expectations and needs and about adjustments you might make.

Decision 4: Voice

"Who am I as I write this review or essay or whatever?" Although the question may seem silly, it really isn't. Your voice is the character, personality, and attitudes you project toward your subject, toward your purpose, and toward your audience. It is the "you" that you have deliberately chosen to express on this occasion.

Your writing voice, like your speaking voice, should be appropriate for the situation in which you find yourself or which you define. You don't use the same voice with your parents that you use with your friend. You don't use the same voice with your professor that you use with your dog. Because we have so much experience speaking, we adopt the appropriate voice almost without thinking about it.

When we begin to write, however, we need to confront these

choices consciously and to weigh a number of factors. Consider this variety of possible attitudes affecting your voice:

Subject: treat it seriously, lightly, humorously, reverently?

Purpose: praise, abuse, ask a favor, explain a process, encourage, persuade, complain?

Audience: peers, enemies, professor, lover, fellow vegetarians, other psychology students?

Occasion: formal, informal, ceremonious?

Clearly, these options are interdependent; that is, a writer probably wouldn't ask a favor in an abusive voice or complain to someone in authority in a humorous one. Your task as a writer is to match the voice to the occasion, the subject, the purpose, and the audience. Many types of writing in psychology have prescribed standards for voice, as we'll see in subsequent chapters.

Just how do you convey a voice, once you've selected one? **Word choice** is one way. To the sensitive writer, most so-called synonyms aren't equal. *Abdicate*, *resign*, *quit*, and *walk out* might mean roughly the same, but they aren't identical in meaning or in voice. Some words are simple and straightforward, others seem more formal. The distinction is made obvious in this pair of sentences that have the same meaning but different voices:

"She purveys Mollusca at the littoral area."
"She sells seashells at the sea shore."

Another stylistic element that conveys voice is **sentence structure.** A long, complex sentence might be more appropriate for a relatively formal treatment of a serious subject for educated readers, whereas a series of short, declarative sentences could be more apt for informal treatment of the same subject and for the same audience.

Even **punctuation** helps establish voice. A semicolon, for example, is a fairly formal mark of punctuation. Writing in an informal voice, you'd be more likely to separate clauses with a period. Dashes and exclamation marks generally have an informal effect. See Chapter 11 for other punctuation guidelines.

Voice, audience, purpose, and subject — these are the key prewriting decisions. Making knowledgeable choices about each — that is your job as writer.

> WRITING 1.4: DEFINING VOICE. Explain what voice you think would be appropriate for each of your responses in Writing 1.3. Be specific and state how concerns of subject and purpose affect your decision.

TECHNIQUES FOR GETTING STARTED

So far in this chapter we've spent a good deal of time talking about what writing does or can do, with little attention to how you actually produce it. Despite the best of intentions, it often seems difficult to get started on a writing assignment. You may feel that all you have is a jumble of ideas and you don't know how to begin to assemble them on paper. So you get another cup of coffee or play one more game of trivia. Or perhaps you feel that your mind is a blank; you don't have any ideas at all for the assignment. So you keep putting it off — avoid thinking about it — maybe inspiration will suddenly appear in the midst of a TV show.

Just how should you get started on a writing project? Is it best to make a detailed plan of what you wish to say before you begin to write? Or should you jump right into an assignment, let your writing flow, and worry about organization later? There is, of course, no "correct" way to begin a writing exercise. While there are no magic formulas to make writing easier, there are several preliminary steps or exercises which can remove some of the panic and inertia associated with staring at a blank sheet of paper.

1. Focused Free Writing

It's brief. It's painless. No one will ever see it but you. And you can ignore it if it doesn't seem to get you anywhere. Focused free writing involves sitting yourself down with a pencil and paper and forcing yourself to write on your topic rapidly and without judgment for a limited amount of time.

Strachey (1955) argued that the development of Freud's psychoanalytic technique was influenced, in part, by a similar process described in an 1823 essay by Borne. Titling his work, "The Art of Becoming an Original Writer in Three Days," Borne wrote:

> Take a few sheets of paper and for three days on end write down, without fabrication or hypocrisy, everything that comes into your head. Write down what you think of yourself, of your wife, of the Turkish War, of Goethe, of Fonk's trial, of the Last Judgement, of your superiors — and when three days have passed you will be quite out of your senses with astonishment at the new and unheard-of thoughts you have had. This is the art of becoming an original writer in three days (Strachey, 1955, p. 265).

You needn't spend three days on it for free writing to succeed — ten to fifteen minutes will work fine. And don't worry if you feel you have nothing to say. Don't be concerned about writing in a coherent or profound way. Focused free writing is a type of "discovery draft" — a technique to draw out your thinking. Don't try to plan what you're going to write. Don't try to anticipate what will come out of it. Just put your pencil to paper and make yourself write continuously on whatever comes to mind. The only restriction to your writing is that you should stay focused on the topic. Consider this example of one of our student's attempts to get started on an assignment using focused free writing.

> This is so ridiculous. I don't know what's supposed to come out of it. How do I evaluate the "frustration - aggression" hypothesis? I don't think I really even know what it is. Frustration-aggression, frustration-aggression. FRUSTRATION!! I feel frustrated - so I'll rip this paper up! But it all seems so simplistic. How could anyone ever believe that? I mean I <u>do</u> feel frustrated but I'm <u>not</u> tearing this paper <u>up</u> - of course, I'd like <u>to!</u> So is that enough to say I'm being aggressive - because I'd like to, even though I'm not? What is aggression anyway? How can anyone buy the frustration-aggression hypothesis if you don't know what aggression is first? I mean, if you've got to actually <u>act out</u> aggression then maybe frustration only sometimes leads to aggression - kicking your flat tire. But if I feel like being aggressive but I'm not actually doing it, is that aggression? Does the hypothesis say that frustration <u>always</u> leads to

```
aggression? Or is it that aggression can be caused
by frustration, but it isn't always? Or is it that
whenever there's aggression, you know that there's
already been some frustration? I don't know.
```

Just what has this student accomplished? At first glance it may not appear to be much. But reconsider. She begins the free write by claiming that she doesn't know what the frustration-aggression hypothesis is. Meanwhile she discovers that she actually does have some ideas of what it might be — she needs to check these out. Her writing reveals an emotional reaction to the subject: "It all seems so simplistic." So she *does* have some feelings about the topic after all, and that's a start. In fact, her reaction suggests that she has already been evaluating the hypothesis. Now she can further ask herself *why* she feels that way. Her writing helps her identify what she finds confusing about the hypothesis and, at the same time, starts her thinking about the variety of possible relationships between frustration and aggression. Moreover, in this brief exercise she has already begun to identify examples of behavior which don't seem to support the frustration-aggression hypothesis, a key step in evaluation. These preliminary ideas can serve as a framework for subsequently developing and organizing a more formal draft — a process made much easier by having something (anything) down on paper. Free writing is meant as a wellspring for ideas — once you get a few, they tend to generate others. So what has this student accomplished in terms of getting started on her assignment? It's quite a lot for a ten-minute investment.

2. Clustering

Either before or just after you've tried focused free writing, sketch an informal diagram of the themes in your topic. Don't be concerned about being completely systematic. Just start with your main topic, surround it with major issues or questions it brings to mind, then write down the issues those bring to mind, and so on. This technique is called **clustering,** and its purpose is similar to free writing: to help your mind unlock what it already knows about a subject. Like free writing, the clustering exercise will continue to focus your subject. It can also advance your thinking as you begin to

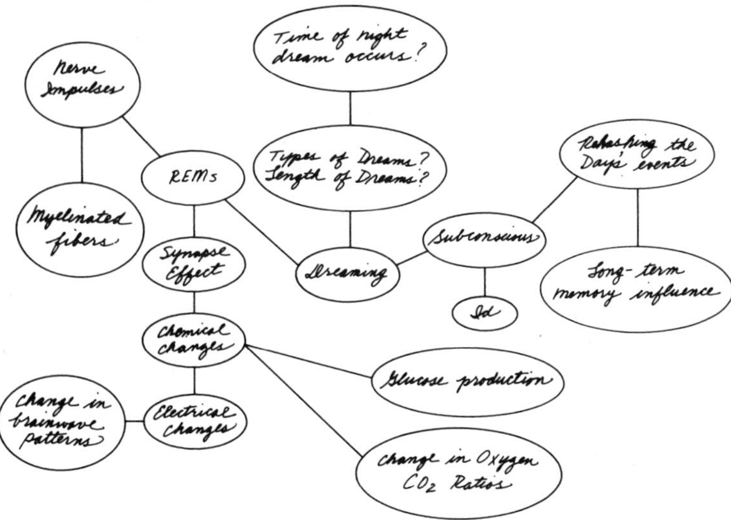

Figure 1.2 *Clustering*

divide and subdivide concepts into categories. Figure 1.2, for example, is one student's attempt to use a clustering exercise for a paper on the physiology of dreaming.

It is clear in this cluster diagram that most of the concepts on the left of the page are more relevant to the topic than those on the right. In fact, now that the student has identified some of the major issues, he can pursue these concepts through library research to determine their actual importance. At any rate, this student has already begun to compose his paper. In the continuing process of prewriting and then drafting, the structure of the paper will undoubtedly change, but this brief sketch, coupled with a few pages of focused free writing, are excellent strategies for moving beyond the blank page and establishing a direction.

3. Talking It Out

Another strategy for discovering your own thoughts is to talk to someone else about your subject. Discuss the project; try to explain your basic ideas. You may find it helpful to speak with your professors, since they often can ask relevant questions and give direction to your thinking. But talking to a friend or a roommate can be just as helpful, if not more so. Those who know little or nothing about your topic may ask about those basic sorts of issues which should lay the groundwork for your essay. Of course, the input from your listener is only part of the benefit of talking it out. Structuring your language through speech will help you become more aware of what you know and don't know, where your logic is clear and where it is fuzzy, which ideas are relevant to your larger thesis and which are not. In fact, you should use this technique throughout the composing process; it's particularly helpful in working through points where you just can't find the "right" words and where a paper has lost its focus.

4. Outlining

Shortly after "talking through" the general design of your essay, try composing a brief outline or table of contents of the major points you expect to cover. Perhaps we tend to cringe at the idea of an outline because of all those associations we have with doing outlines in seventh grade English — it seems like such a tedious, even intimidating, process when we get hung up on the details of its form and content. Well don't! This outline is just for **you,** something to make **your** life easier. Keep the form and content flexible; make it rough, make it loose. It's just a way to begin to establish the direction — and material — you want to cover.

Figure 1.3 has, on the left, an example of an extremely rough, informal "outline" which laid the groundwork for this section of this chapter. On the right is a subsequent revision of the original — still quite informal in form, but more developed in organization.

Our outlines are always subject to dramatic revisions — in the middle of writing we often get new ideas which reshape our original thinking. In fact, making a new outline *after* you've finished a first draft is a good way to check the flow of logic in your writing.

5. Establishing a Rhythm

In an essay entitled "A Writer's Discipline," Jacques Barzun argued that first you must "convince yourself that you are working in clay and not marble, on paper and not eternal bronze: let that first sen-

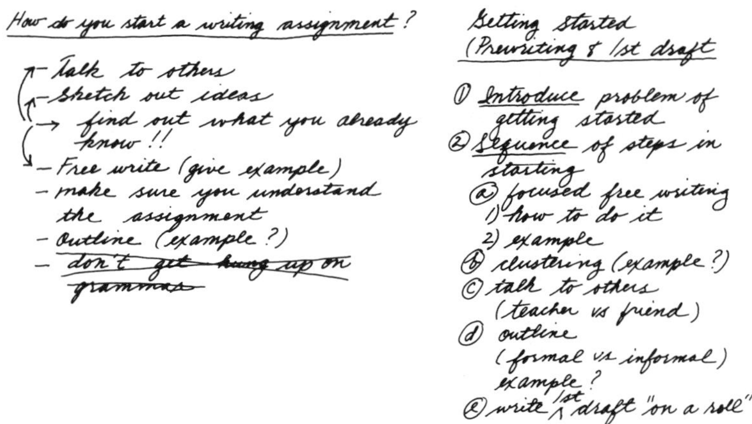

Figure 1.3 *Outlining*

tence be as stupid as it wishes. No one will rush out and print it as it stands. Just put it down; then another" (1971 p. 8). It is crucial to establish a rhythm to your work: If you can't think of the precise word you need in a particular context, continue without it. If you can't think of an appropriate example where it's needed, or are having trouble deciding between two possibilities, just make a note to yourself in the margin, "example" or "learning? conditioning?," and get on with developing the larger analysis. Rule number one in writing and in Las Vegas: Never stop when you are on a roll.

Don't agonize over spelling or grammatical rules. These issues are better left for later revisions or, in the case of an essay exam, when you are ready to proofread your answer. During the composing process it helps to permit your language to flow as rapidly as possible. This is especially true in an essay exam when you are working against the constraints of time, but it is also the case for more leisurely writing. As you establish a momentum, you start to gain a sense of confidence. You begin to realize how much you actually know about your subject, discover possibilities for organizing the information and, just as important, decide what issues you need to think about further. When you reread your first draft, you will undoubtedly discover elements of repetition and moments of utter incoherency. But don't attempt to reconstruct or polish the material until you are satisfied that you have stated the core idea(s). Why bother "perfecting" a sentence before you're certain it belongs there? Most of all, to return to Barzun's (1971) argument, just get your thinking into language, regardless of how rough the beast initially appears. Not even the most accomplished writers produce first drafts that say exactly what they intend.

In spite of all of this, our guess is that many people would prefer to ignore all we've said. It's so tempting to try to write a first and final draft from scratch, because the very idea of revising sounds long and tedious. But think about the time you've wasted staring at a blank page or getting up for a snack, a drink, or whatever, because of the difficulty in getting started. The process of focused free writing, clustering, talking, outlining, drafting, and revising is sometimes actually quicker, and certainly more coherent and productive, than trying to compose the final product from scratch.

WRITING 1.5: GETTING STARTED. Develop the foundation of a brief (1–2 page) but solid essay. Choose a topic you have covered in your course that interests you, perhaps enlarging upon a promising journal entry. For example, you might consider the causes of conformity or the impact of school failure on self-esteem. First use focused free writing and clustering, and then talk it out with a friend. Then outline (or even list) the sequence of points you hope to cover, and draft the essay (remembering to keep it rolling). Now you should have the basis for a potentially fine essay — perhaps not the first time you try this sequence, but after some practice.

[2] *Using a Journal*

TOBY FULWILER

PREVIEW:

12/9/85 Okay. Although I just read this article I still don't understand why people join "cults." So — we all have to grow up & deal with maturity — why do these kids w/ strong middle class families turn away from them? What is this "empty" stuff? If every time I felt low self-esteem or empty, I would be running a cult right now. Somehow it seems like a cop-out.

Maybe it's because these kids don't feel as if they can talk to their parents about their insecurities. I don't know. Obviously I'm not an expert — but I always felt that my playing on athletic teams was almost therapeutic. I always felt that the sport pulled us together & when I was out on the field my family, emotional, academic, & financial problems were temporarily left in the locker room . . . Well maybe my putting my field hockey uniform on & shoving my hair in a pony tail was like wearing a red cloak & shaving my head.

—Student Journal Entry

This chapter shows how a journal can help you think and write about psychology. Journals, as you may know, are places to record observations, speculate, raise questions, and, in general, figure things out. In the journal entry above, for instance, we see a sophomore recording her first reactions to a reading assignment about cults: At first she cannot understand why anyone would join a cult, but as she writes further, she begins to find a connection between her own participation in athletics and the psychological needs which lead to cult membership. Journals are places in which to explore personal connections to academic subjects, in your own words, and to yourself.

Journals have been used in a similar manner throughout history by serious thinkers, writers, scientists, psychologists, artists, philosophers, and teachers — people for whom it is important to capture and record their thoughts. St. Augustine and Jean-Jacques Rousseau based their "confessions" on journals. Most of our Founding Fathers kept journals, as did authors such as Ralph Waldo Emerson and Henry David Thoreau — whose natural observations led to great literature. So did the major psychological thinkers of our time: Freud, Jung, Skinner, and Piaget, for example. Samuel Pepys, Anaïs Nin, and Virginia Woolf, all writers, called their journals "diaries." Edward Weston, the photographer, called his a "daybook." Albert Camus, philosopher and writer, called his simply a "notebook." Still others have called them "logs," or "commonplace books." Of course, it doesn't matter what you call them. What matters is that we understand why these forms of personal writing are useful and how they work.

If you have never kept a journal, you might have some questions: What, exactly, is a journal? What does one look like? If I do keep one, what and when should I write in it? Above all, what can it do for me in this class? How can it possibly help me learn more about psychology? Let's look at some answers.

WHAT IS A JOURNAL?

I can give you an easy explanation first: Journals assigned in class are essentially one part diary and one part course notebook. But a journal is also distinctly different from each. Diaries record the private thoughts and experiences of the writer. Class notebooks usually record the public thoughts and presentations of the teacher. The journal is somewhere between the two. Like the diary, the journal is written in the first person (I) about ideas important to the writer, but like the class notebook, the journal focuses on academic subjects the writer wants to think more about. You could represent journals this way:

Diary →	Journal ←	Class Notebook
("I")	("I/it")	("it")

Journals may be focused narrowly on the subject matter of a psychology, literature, or philosophy course, or broadly on the whole range of your academic and personal experience. Each journal entry is a deliberate exercise in expansion: "How far can I take this idea? How accurately can I describe or explain it? How can I make it make sense to me?" The journal encourages you to become conscious, through language, of what is happening around you, both personally and academically.

CHARACTERISTICS OF JOURNALS

What's unique about journals is that they convey thought trapped in time. They are organized quite differently than more traditional assignments. "Chronology" rather than "theme" provides the unity, and this sets them apart from many other academic compositions. But while single journal entries are locked together in time, the whole collection may transcend time to reveal more complex, often lucid, patterns of growth and understanding over the course of a semester. Journals become histories of evolving thought. Unlike formal papers, journals carry with them all the time-bound fragments of thought that would otherwise be discarded, modified, or forgotten.

Language, too, sets journals apart. Some of the characteristics of good journal writing may run directly counter to traditional notions about appropriate academic writing, as the example at the beginning of this chapter showed. (We'll look at more samples shortly.) Journals may be full of sentence fragments, digressions, dashes instead of semicolons, frequent references to oneself (I), misspellings, shorthand, doodles, sloppy handwriting, self-doubt, and all sorts of unexplained private references and notations. These features, however, which can be both distracting and enlightening at the same time, occur in journals for different reasons than they occur in more formal writing. Journal writers must feel free to write in their most comfortable, fast, close-at-hand style at all times. As a result, good journal writing is usually more fun to read — more like personal letters — than more traditional, perhaps overly formal, academic prose. The more we trust the value of our own informal voice, in fact, the more we will use it to both generate and communicate ideas.

Use your journal as a place in which to think, reflect, experiment, and play with language. And try to make it a habit. Journals are private places where talking to oneself becomes legitimate. Don't be afraid to take some risks with form, style, and voice. (In academic journals, when something becomes too private or risky, simply pull it out when you turn your journal in to your teacher.) Notice how writing in the early morning differs from writing late at night. Experience how writing at the same time every day, regardless of inclination or mood, often produces surprising results.

Above all else, your journal is a place where you can be honest with yourself (and your teacher), so write in the language that comes easiest to you. Here, for example, is an entry written for a child psychology class; the student did not have her journal with her and so made this entry on a napkin in a shopping mall:

> 10/15 Sitting here in the University Mall – Yuck! So why am I here? Oh well, anything beats the monotony of school once in a while. Anyway, I can't believe the way the mummies treat the kiddies around here. Yell, yell, yell. Hell! But here I am sipping coke and right next to me is this mother whose kid seems to be <u>trying</u> to make her yell, but she won't. I mean, it's not like the mom is being nice instead. She just won't respond to <u>anything</u> the kid does. So is this an improvement? What's the kid to think?? I wonder if this is any better than yelling? Maybe it's worse!

This entry is not written in the formal academic style; instead, it's written in the writer's more comfortable, talky, personal language, which helps the writer catch her thoughts and mood fast — thoughts here which lead to personal insights about mothering —

and which could lead to researchable questions for her field of study. In journals, the language is your own.

WHY KEEP A JOURNAL?

The act of writing helps people understand things better. If you are a student of psychology and you write about theories, data, concepts, and problems associated with human behavior, you will begin to sort out those issues more clearly. *Any* assignment can be made richer by reflecting about it *to yourself* in your journal or notebook: How do I feel about this? What do I care about? What do I know? What don't I know? What do I want to know? What have I forgotten that I might remember if I wrote about it?

Writing helps you both sort out and retrieve all sorts of information, ideas, and impressions already existing somewhere in your head. Notice what happens when you write letters to friends — how you often begin writing with one thing on your mind and then surprise yourself by writing about all sorts of other things. The same thing often happens even when you write from an outline — you actually start digressing and going somewhere you never intended. That's one of the remarkable powers of written language; it doesn't just reflect or communicate your thinking, it actually *leads* it! In other words, writing is a powerful way of thinking.

And sometimes writing tells you flatly where you can't go that you thought you could! As you try to explain yourself, you sometimes discover holes you didn't see before and recognize that you need more information or a different way of thinking about the topic. Learning when you're about to step onto thin ice can be a real survival skill — better to find that out in a private journal than in a public paper or examination. In a journal, you have time to do something about it: read more, research more, ask more questions. Writing in journals about what you don't know is one of the best ways to start knowing.

Your journal will be a place to think and a tool to think with. Use it to monitor class progress, to write daily plans, to rehearse for class discussion, to practice for examinations, and as a seedbed from which to generate research and term papers. Class notebooks can be turned into journals when writers speculate on the meaning of someone else's information and ideas. Reflections about psychological issues help you to not only identify with and make sense of what you have read in textbooks and listened to in class lectures, but also to understand your own life, growth, and development. Likewise, trial hypotheses about social, economic, intellectual, or political behavior might find first articulation in this same journal. Continued writing about theoretical ideas can develop those ideas into full-fledged research designs.

SUGGESTIONS FOR KEEPING JOURNALS

The following list provides ideas for starting and keeping academic journals in virtually any college subject area. But remember, these are just suggestions, not commandments. In truth, journals can look like and be anything you or your professor wishes.

1. Buy a looseleaf notebook; this will allow you to add and subtract entries as you wish.

2. Divide it into three sections: class entries, readings, and personal questions. This will help you keep track of various threads of thought and could be especially useful if you write entries for several classes in the same semester.

3. Date each entry, including time of day. Chronology is the distinguishing mark of journals and lets you watch your own thoughts change over time.

4. Write in your most comfortable, informal style; this will help you relax and concentrate more on your thought than on style.

5. Write regularly, daily if possible. The habit of regular writing simply increases your chances of finding new ideas or developing old ones more fully.

6. Write long entries, a new full page each time. Again, this increases your chances of discovering thoughts as you begin to have a dialogue with yourself.

7. Collect quotes, clippings, scraps of interest. Here, the jour-

nal can help you keep things worth remembering in one place in chronological order for future use or pleasure.

8. At the end of the term, add page numbers, titles for each entry, table of contents, and an introduction. This guarantees that you review your own record of thought and, at the same time, makes it easier for your professor to read.

WHAT TO WRITE

Journals can contain any or all modes of thought and expression which can be written or diagrammed. However, they are especially useful for encouraging the very modes of thought most valued in the academic community. The following suggestions may give you some ideas for things to try out in your journal:

1. Observation. Use the journal to record, in your own language, what you see. The simplest observations are sensory experiences. They may be primarily visual, but also aural, tactile, and the like, and are particularly useful when visiting a place, watching people, or recording data. Here, for example, is an entry from another student observing a child's behavior:

> 9/21 I saw an infant today waiting in a lunch line . . . I can't believe I started to notice all the things he did. The baby would pull at its mother's hair for attention . . . then start gazing at all the people and objects. He would smile at the person behind his mother . . . and then his glance would move to something else. His fingers were always in his mouth, and when his mother tried to pull them out and wipe them . . . five minutes later they were back in.

The key to good observation is being there, finding words to capture what you witness, and being able to experience it again when you see it recorded. In psychology, as in most academic subjects, observation is a crucial way to collect data. Piaget, for example, based much of his theory of cognitive development on personal observations of his family, which he recorded. Journals let you both collect and think about what you have collected. Look for details, examples, measurements, analogies, and descriptive language that includes color, texture, size, shape, and movement.

2. Speculation. Use your journal to wonder "What if?" Speculation, in fact, is the essence of good journals, perhaps the very reason for their existence and importance. Journals allow writers to speculate freely and even wildly without fear of penalty. Use your journal to think hard about possibilities — no penalties here for free thinking or imagining. Here, for example, are a few lines from a page-long entry in response to a lecture on "Learned Helplessness":

> 10/1 I often wonder how much of what a child's childhood is like really affects his/her adult life. In going over my thoughts on this lecture, I wonder if this feeling of "I have no effect on my environment" affects the adult person?

In this case, the journal writer made a note next to the entry which read "possible research." This student did, in fact, turn this initial speculation into a full-scale research paper later in the term.

3. Questions. Sometimes writers use journals to record their doubts and uncertainties — one of the few places in the academic world where such frank admissions of ignorance have a place. (It may be all right to admit orally, after class, that you don't know an answer or understand something; it is something else altogether to admit that on an examination or formal essay.) Journal writers expect to write about what they don't know as well as what they do know. Another name for a journal? A doubt book. Don't be afraid to write "What's that supposed to mean?" and "I just don't get this." In fact, in journals, it's as important to ask such questions as to answer them. Questions indicate that something is happening — in this case, that there may be some disequilibrium or uncertainty in your mind, and that you are willing to explore it through language. Again, the ability to *see* one's questions helps sharpen, clarify, and understand them better. And once you are aware of exactly what it is you don't understand, you can begin to try to explore and resolve the issues. In the following entry, we see a student raising questions triggered by a teacher's assertion in class:

```
9/17 Just how wrong were Aristotle and John Locke
with their notions of a ''Tabula Rasa,'' or blank
slate? Of course, we all know that children are not
born without genetic programming, but just how im-
portant is this genetic programming in infant
development?
```

Some questions will stick close to the course content and others will stray into the writer's personal life; in journals, both are important to the writer's social and intellectual development. Here is an example of how an entry bridges the gap between the writer's academic and personal life:

```
12/10 Brain Food. I can definitely relate to that
article. I for one know that I do not intake or get
enough vitamins or nutrients. Plus I do not think
that I eat properly either. According to the arti-
cle, the results of this sort of behavior are anxi-
ety, depression, insomnia. I happen to experience
all of these symptoms . . . I wonder if a deter-
mined effort to take B vitamins would help?
```

4. Awareness. Learn who you are, record where you are, think about where you want to go. Be conscious of yourself as a learner, thinker, or writer. Self-awareness is necessary for both higher-order reasoning and mature social interactions. Journals are places where writers can actually monitor and witness the evolution of self-awareness. You can encourage yourself to become more aware by asking lots of questions and trying out lots of answers: "What am I learning in here? What do I remember about today's lecture or reading? What has any of this got to do with reality? With me? Why do I want to study psychology, anyway? The entry about nutrition in the previous section or the entry with which this chapter began are also good examples of self-awareness promoted by keeping a journal.

5. Connections. Use the journal to try to make the study of any academic subject relevant to everything else in your life. Can you make connections? Force connections? Find easy connections? Connections to other courses or other events in your life? Journals encourage such connecting because no one is insisting that writers stick to one organized, well-documented subject. Connections can be loose or tight, tangential or direct; the point is, they are connections made by the writer (you), not somebody else. Digressions are also connections. They indicate that something is happening to trigger your memory, to bring forth information and ideas stored in your long-term memory. In journals, they are valuable. Here are some fragments from psychology journals which indicate that connections are being made:

> 9/25 I'm taking a course in the education department . . . and the class stresses a certain point that I found prominent in this chapter. . . .

> 12/5 When Babbit was mentioned in the explanation of fear of life it got the old wheels turning. In my U.S. History class much reference was made to that book . . .

> 10/27 I saw, on "60 Minutes" tonight, a segment that reminded me of the article we read in September called ''The Origins of Life''. . . .

Connections occur when you begin to see one subject in terms of another; the study of psychology *is* related to the study of philosophy, religion, the arts, and so on. Journals help you put together the many pieces of a liberal arts education.

6. Dialogue. Talk to your teacher through the journal. Have a conversation, find out some things about each other — things perhaps too tangential or personal for class, but which build relationships all the same. Consider this journal as "dialogical." Do not expect complete candor from each other, but do expect some honest give-and-take. Journals can help you learn more about each other if you share entries from time to time, either out loud in class or privately through written responses in the journal itself.

7. Information. Collect and comment on everything you can find that relates to your course of study. Ironically, the straight factual information in a journal may seem like the least interesting material you collect. Usually it serves more as a record than anything else. A former student copied undigested reading notes in his journal, ended up calling them "Cliff Notes stuff," and wished he had put it in a class notebook and not his journal. However, such references — especially when connected with some personal reaction — supply writers with valuable insights about otherwise rather distant material. In a psychology class, for instance, you might create a special section of your journal and label it "Topics for Further Investigation," where you collect ideas run across in readings or travels. Such topics can provide ideas for research and study in the future; the journal is a natural place to keep them. In a journal, though, unlike a class notebook, be sure to record information in your own words. This will increase your chances of understanding and remembering these ideas. Here's an example of a student simply rehearsing class information in his journal:

> 10/5 It is interesting how in human development, every aspect seems to start egocentric or physically from the center. . . . This same pattern seems to repeat itself time & time again throughout the first ten years or so of life. First physical growth -- starts at head to trunk to extremities. Motor growth -- head & neck, gross movements to finer finger dexterity.

8. Revision. Consider your journal as a place in which to rethink ideas. Try looking back in your journal to see if you can locate where you have since changed your mind about something. Then write about what you now think and why you changed your mind. Anne Berthoff, a professor at the University of Massachusetts, advocates what she calls a "double-entry notebook," in which writers return periodically to reflect upon previous entries (1978). In other words, build opportunities for revision into the journal itself. Leaving generous margins or some space after each entry helps or, in a looseleaf notebook, you can simply add new pages. At other times, consider the journal as a place in which to start formal papers — to make several starts — until one idea begins to develop a life of its own. Then go with that one — as far as you can until it busts loose from your journal altogether. This is a good way of generating first drafts. In the following entry a student rethinks his ideas about the imitation theory of language learning:

> 10/24 I just reread the entry I made 10/21 and new ideas popped into my head. Imitation may be a worn out theory concerning acquisition of language in a

```
normal baby: what about deaf children? They can't
imitate the sounds they hear because they can't
hear . . . I guess that it's a mixture of theories
& that the mixture is weighted differently for each
person.
```

9. Problem Posing and Solving. Use your journal to pose as well as solve problems related to psychology. Just as questioning and speculating are natural in journals, so too is actually setting out on your own to find solutions. Don't make the posing something only teachers and experts do; use your journal to help here. Whether the problem is posed well, or whether the solution actually works, matters little. (If the problems are consistently ill defined and the solutions always off base, that does matter, but here, the journal will be invaluable in another way — as an early clue to where you are really having trouble.) According to Brazilian educator, Paulo Friere (1970), individuals must articulate problems in their own language in order to experience significant growth. Journals are, perhaps, the best place in the academic world in which to do that. Evidence of posing and solving problems — whether psychological, literary, social, scientific, or mechanical — suggests that you're alive, thoughtful, and involved, and will be a useful person in any industry or business.

In college, of course, problems may be of a different nature: taking tests, locating paper topics, and actually writing the papers. Using a journal can help you with each of these. Many students have discovered term paper topics simply by rereading their journals: A single entry often becomes a whole series of entries on a particular subject area, a good indication that a solid foundation exists upon which to build more formal research. In fact, some teachers assign questions to ponder in the journal which they intend to return to periodically in the course. The following entry suggests how journals might help solve these problems:

```
10/25  I found that the journal entries were help-
ful because they started you on the writing track,
and by doing entries I gained information and a
sense of what I wanted to write in the final paper.
```

10. Synthesis. One of the best and most practical activities to do with your journal is to synthesize, daily and weekly, what's going on in your study of psychology: "How does this lecture relate to the last one? What do I expect next time? How does class discussion relate to the stated objectives on the syllabus?" Your written answers to any of these questions can easily generate comments to share with both class and teacher. If you can take even five minutes at the end of each discussion or lecture — or stay in your seat five minutes after class — you can catch perceptions and connections that will otherwise escape as you run off to another class, lunch, or a quick snooze back at your room. Journals invite you to put together what you learn. In the following entry, we see the kind of synthesis possible when, near the end of the term, ideas from several sources begin to come together:

> 12/7 "Children of Divorce." Both from this article and from class lecture about divorce and its impact on children, it seems to me that it is not so much the divorce per se that is damaging as it is what the divorce brings about in terms of changes in routine and feelings/relationships between the adult(s) and the child(ren). Maybe that seems like such an obvious statement . . . but it wasn't obvious to me.

FIELD AND LABORATORY NOTEBOOKS

In psychology, as in the natural sciences, your instructor may ask you to keep a very particular kind of journal called a "Field" or "Laboratory Notebook." Such a document is actually a kind of cross between a journal and a notebook, written with the deliberate attempt to (1) note the procedural details of each experimental session or observation period, (2) record all data from whatever experiment or situation one is observing, and (3) keep a running record of speculations and questions about those observations. In such notebooks dates, times, places, and site conditions are crucial for later work in laboratory, study or library. A field or laboratory notebook does very much the same things a journal does, but is more focused in its intention. Chapter 7, the Research Report, elaborates on the use of a lab notebook.

SUMMARY

Let's conclude this chapter by looking at a student's reaction to the role the journal played in her psychology class:

> 12/11 One final entry before the end of Psych 161 is over: I must say that, more than any other class, this class has stressed to me . . . the fact that writing does promote thinking. I have really enjoyed getting my thoughts down on paper. And even when I didn't think I had any thoughts relevant to the subject at hand . . . before I knew it, I had written an entire page. Writing helped me sort out my thoughts and to apply the concepts I was learning in the text/readings etc. to previous experiences in my childhood &/or adolescence. The journal was a good place to INTEGRATE all the material that the course entailed, a place in which to "fit the pieces of the puzzle together" and get a more complete, well-rounded, whole picture of the course. The funny thing was that the more I kept writing, the more I found that I was able to do this and really understand this integration . . . incidently, I also feel that talking and walking promote thinking.

If you let journal writing work for you in some of the ways suggested in this chapter, I think you'll gradually learn to be both a better learner and a better writer. Journals aren't magic. But the practice of daily speculative writing will exercise your mind in much the same way that running or swimming exercises your body. The practice of writing to oneself can become a useful regular habit: Try fifteen minutes each morning with coffee, twenty minutes each evening before homework, or even ten minutes before bed. You will find writing in it easier and easier and, in time, may find it a mentally restful activity — the one time in a busy schedule to put your life in order. And at the end of the term or after you graduate you'll find this marvelous written record of your thoughts, beliefs, problems, solutions, and dreams. Journal writing is a powerful process that results in a wonderfully personal product.

[3] Writing Exams and Short Essay Assignments

PREVIEW:

Preliminary Considerations

What Kind of Information Should My Answer Provide?

What Form Should My Answer Take?

What Is the Purpose of the Question?

Common Types of Information Requests

Definition

Classification

Analysis

Comparison/Contrast

Argument/Evaluation

Trial by Fire: Writing Under Time Pressure

PRELIMINARY CONSIDERATIONS

"We've just got a midterm and a final exam, and neither includes long essays. Writing isn't really required in this class." That's a common misconception. Although many students may recognize that writing plays an important role in long essays, papers, etc., they often assume that the writing process is only tangential to their efforts on exams and brief essay assignments. But, in fact, even fill-in-the-blank questions, short identifications, and definitions involve an important writing component. Think about it for a moment. If you are given only three words or perhaps one sentence in which to respond, you have to be particularly careful to select brief, accurate, and well-organized words or phrases. In short answers, you don't have the luxury of rephrasing and reexplaining your ideas. You must think and write in a very concise and integrative way.

Perhaps you'll admit that exams and essay assignments *are* writing assignments. But you may have also insisted that it is unfair to be graded on your writing. After all, this is a psychology course, not an English course. The fact is that writing is a form of thinking, learning, and communication, and that's what exams and other essay assignments are all about. They are designed both to promote and to assess your understanding of a field. In writing exams and essays in general, you typically are asked to think about your own thinking, and then to develop, organize, and communicate those thoughts to someone else (usually the professor). Therefore, whether you like it or not, it's literally impossible to separate *what* you say from *how* you say it. Here are some preliminary questions you need to ask when responding to exams or essay assignments.

What Kind of Information Should My Answer Provide?

You confidently hand in an assignment or exam after writing a long and detailed answer. You feel good about knowing the material. The following week the assignment is returned with a mediocre grade and a comment in bright red, "YOU DIDN'T ANSWER THE QUESTION!" This can be incredibly frustrating.

The first rule of thumb in approaching any writing assignment is to read the question carefully and **identify the requirements** of the question. This sounds like such obvious advice, but it is amazing how rarely we actually take the time to follow it. Ask yourself quite consciously, "What is the specific kind of information that is being requested?" Are you being asked to **define** a word or concept? Are you being asked to provide an **example** of a word or concept? Is your task to **compare** two different positions or theories? Or are you to **argue** or **evaluate** a position? The point is that despite the quantity of information you may provide, and even the quality of that information, your response will be judged in terms of how well it answers the specific question being asked.

Consider the exam situation in which a class was asked to "describe the relationship between perception and cognition." David T. responded:

```
Cognition is the process of knowing; it concerns
the way information is represented, organized, and
transformed to influence our behavior. Perception
```

> is the process we use to get firsthand information about the world; it involves our awareness of activities that are currently occurring in our immediate surroundings and our discriminative, selective response to these stimuli.

At first glance this seems to be a nice solid response. David has carefully, concisely, and accurately defined each of the concepts. But, unfortunately, he has not done what he was asked — to "**describe the relationship** between perception and cognition." He has instead approached the question as if it were a request for definitions. No matter how accurate and complete his answer, he has failed to provide an analysis of a relationship, as was requested. Compare this with Sara M.'s response:

> Perception is the process by which we experience ongoing environmental stimulation firsthand. It involves the way we selectively discriminate between and respond to these stimuli. Cognition refers to the more general process of knowing. It involves the way we process, organize, represent, and interpret information, which in turn affects our behavior. Therefore, perception is the first step in the process of cognition. Experiencing the presence of stimuli is a first step in coming to know our world. Our immediate perceptions make up part of that which we process, organize, represent, and interpret (i.e., cognition). Meanwhile, some psychologists have argued that perception and cognition have mutual effects upon each other. Not only do our perceptions affect how we think about and organize information (cognition), but our general process of knowing and interpreting information seems to affect the ways in which we process our immediate environment (perception).

While Sara began her response by providing definitions (which were quite similar to David's), she used them simply to set the stage for the main part of her answer, the **analysis of the relationship** between perception and cognition (the portion we've underlined).

In just a moment we'll take a more systematic look at the different kinds of questions which are typically asked and the special requirements of each. For now, just keep in mind that, regardless of the writing context, you have to identify the specific kind(s) of information requested before you respond.

What Form Should My Answer Take?

As we talk about specific writing assignments in other chapters, we will emphasize the format and style requirements of those tasks. Although general essays and exam questions do not have standardized format requirements, any one question or assignment may ask for a particular form of response. Sometimes the **content** of a response seems relatively independent of its **form.** That is, **what** you say does not seem particularly affected by the overall format of your response. For instance, let's say you are asked to explain three examples of a defense mechanism. It's probably of little importance whether you list your examples and explanations or embed them in a paragraph. At other times, however, the **form** is quite relevant to the purpose or function of an assignment and is crucial to shaping the content of the answer, as is the case with an abstract. Therefore, when approaching any question or assignment, identify not only the kind of information being requested, but also the form which it should take.

What Is the Purpose of the Question?

There may be a variety of reasons a particular question or assignment is presented. Identifying its **purpose** will help you to write a better response. For example, the goal of a question may be to test your **memory** of material presented in class or in your readings (e.g., "Name two different theories of gender role development"). Or the purpose of a question may be to assess your **understanding** of the material (e.g., "Explain [that is, give the **meaning** or **interpretation** of] two different theories of gender role development"). On the other hand, a particular question may be designed to assess your ability to **integrate** material from class and/or your readings (e.g., "Explain what you perceive to be the major similarities and differences between the two major theories of gender role development"). Or a question may be designed to look at your ability to **extrapolate** from the course material (e.g., "Based on what you have learned about the two major theories of gender role development, what kinds of predictions would you make about the personality characteristics of children who are raised in single-parent households?").

To summarize, we've suggested that as you prepare to write any assignment, including exam questions and essays, you first ask yourself:

1. What **kind** of information is being requested?
2. What **form** of information is called for by the question?
3. What is the **purpose** of the question?

As you proceed, you'll find that the answers to these questions are not totally independent of one another. For example, the purpose of the question may shape the kind of information being asked for and/or the form in which the answer is to be given. On the other hand, two questions which have a similar purpose (e.g., assessing ability to integrate material) may require different kinds and/or forms of information.

COMMON TYPES OF INFORMATION REQUESTS

Let's focus upon the different types of information which essays and exam questions commonly require. We'll consider briefly the special requirements of each and the role which each plays in our thinking process. You'll find that these are the same kinds of questions and structures we use in virtually all of our writing, whether it be composing a letter to a friend, working on a major term paper, or writing in a diary about a lost love.

Definition

Definitions respond to the question, "What is it?" For example, "define a primary reinforcer" or "explain the meaning of a primary reinforcer" are two questions asking for definitions. How should you proceed?

First, be certain to identify the entire scope of your subject. Many students make the mistake of defining only a portion of the subject. One student responded that a primary reinforcer is "any event or object whose presentation increases the likelihood that the behavior that preceded it will reoccur." That's not a bad definition of "reinforcer," but it ignores some of the specific characteristics of a *primary* reinforcer. Another student answered that a primary reinforcer is "a reinforcer that doesn't have to be learned. It's something that's *naturally* reinforcing." Clearly he was focusing upon the distinction between primary vs. secondary and conditioned reinforcers without ever really defining **reinforcer.** The best definition of "primary reinforcer" would be a combination of the two above, one that considers the intersection of the two terms, for example: "A primary reinforcer is any event or object whose presentation increases the likelihood that the behavior that preceded it will reoccur, and whose effect is not dependent upon previous conditioning."

Second, give some examples of the concept. These illustrations will help to distinguish it for your reader. However, while providing a list of examples may be useful both in guiding your own thinking and in communicating your ideas, a mere list of examples alone, no matter how long, is not generally sufficient to define a concept.

You'll find that definitions serve a very important function in the composition of any kind of essay or paper. They are an excellent means of introducing a topic and assuring that your reader understands the framework in which you're working. Therefore, it's often useful to define key concepts at the beginning of your essay. "Operational definitions" have an almost sacred position in scientific writing. They involve defining a concept in terms of the operations used to measure it. We'll discuss them further when we consider writing literature reviews and research reports (Chapters 5, 6, and 7).

> WRITING 3.1: DEFINITIONS. Select a concept which you have studied in psychology. List 4–5 examples of the concept, then **define** the concept itself. Finally, check to see that your examples and definition agree. If not, revise your definition or reassess your choice of examples.

Classification

Classification questions ask, "What is the overall structure or pattern?" For example, "classify the types of interpersonal relationships which strongly affect adolescent social development" is a classification question. Where do you begin? First, **identify the universe** or scope of your sample. In our example, this step gets us to think about the different sorts of people who shape the adolescent's social development. We might include nagging parents, sensational coaches, hostile peers, lovers, movie stars, overly demanding teachers, supportive parents, rock stars, admiring young siblings, etc. Second, **consider the possible bases** for classifying the members of your universe or sample, defining the characteristics of these potential classes. This step gets you to think about the relationships which exist among the members you have identified, and to select the classification system which seems most meaningful. In answering the hypothetical question above, we could classify the adolescent's interpersonal relationships in a variety of ways, for example, in terms of the sex of the persons involved (male or female), the ages of the persons involved (peers, young adults, middle-aged adults, etc.), or the different roles individuals represent for the adolescent (confidants, realistic role models, idols, targets for defiance, etc.). Clearly the last choice seems most meaningful since it provides insight into why these individuals were originally included in our universe. The final step is to **assign the members** of the universe to the classes defined. Consider the ways in which the individual members actually fit into the larger system we constructed. Lovers and supportive parents might be classified as confidants; nagging parents, overly demanding teachers, and hostile peers might be classified as targets for defiance, etc. This process of assigning members to their respective categories may also reveal an inadequacy in our classification system. (Admiring young siblings don't fit into any of the classes we've identified; therefore, we need to rethink our classes.)

The process of classification often pushes us to think about material in both new and more subtle ways. It is obvious that nagging parents and overly demanding teachers affect the adolescent's development. But by being forced to consider the alternative bases for classifying these and other influences, you derive a new understanding of the functions which these forces serve: targets for defiance. Classification demands careful analysis of the organization or structure of the system. At the same time, it creates a framework for further analysis by considering the parts in relation to the whole.

Analysis

Questions of analysis ask about the relationships between the parts and the whole. For example, if you are asked to "analyze Piaget's stages of cognitive development," you must consider the components of Piaget's stage model. The process of thinking about a concept in terms of its components gives you a greater understanding of the organization and functioning of the whole. There are several different types of analyses, and each asks a different question about the part/whole relationship. Consider each of the following:

1. Analysis of **structure** asks, "What are the parts that make up the whole, and how are they organized?" For example, "explain the sequence of stages of cognitive development, according to Piaget" asks for an analysis of structure. You might respond that, "During the first two years of life, the infant is in the sensory/motor stage; during the preschool years the child functions at the preoperational stage; during the elementary school years the child thinks at the concrete operational level; and during adolescence and adulthood the individual functions at the formal operational stage."

2. Analysis of **function** asks, "What do the parts do?" That is, consider the role which each part serves in relation to the whole. Following our example of Piaget's stages of cognitive development, we might explain that, "sensory/motor intelligence allows only thinking through doing. Infants can process events only in terms of their immediate, concrete experiences. In contrast, preoperational intelligence involves the use of mental representation, and thus the ability to think about things (i.e., mentally represent things) in their absence. Concrete operational intelligence involves not only the use of mental representation but also the use of mature mental operations. The individual is not only able to think about (imagine) things in their absence, but can also manipulate those images, mentally reverse them, place them in a logical, hierarchical network, etc. Formal operational intelligence . . ."

3. Analysis of **process** asks, "How do the parts work together?" That is, consider the interrelationship of their operations. Here, we might explain that "each stage of development appears to

be a necessary precursor for the development of the next; each comprises the foundation for constructing the next. As the individual develops, the 'earlier' forms of intelligence are not lost. In fact, there are many circumstances in which those 'earlier' forms may be more useful and adaptive than the 'later' forms. . . ."

4. Analysis of **cause** asks, "What makes it (or leads it to) work in a particular way?" The process of causal analysis might lead us to consider the interaction of genes, maturation, and environment, and the way in which this interaction produces the sequential construction and use of new levels of cognition.

5. Analysis of **effect** asks, "What is the outcome of its operation?" Here we might consider the ways in which each cognitive developmental stage is believed to shape the individual's social experiences. Analyses of effect get us to think about the implications of our subject's operation.

Thus, the processes involved in analyses lay the groundwork for a comprehensive and in-depth understanding of a concept. By identifying its components, considering what, where, why, and how they operate, and their results, we get a fuller appreciation of the concept. Moreover, such analyses provide an extensive framework for considering the similarities, dissimilarities, and relationships between this concept and others.

WRITING 3.2: ANALYSIS. Return to the concept you defined in Writing 3.1. Draft a brief **analysis** of its structure, function, process, cause, and effect. Note the different kinds of questions addressed by each of these.

WRITING 3.3: CLASSIFICATION. Based upon one of the levels of analysis (function, for example), **classify** the components or examples of the concept. Remember to identify the members of your universe, identify a basis for classifying your members, and then assign your members to your classes. Explore whether there is an alternative basis for classification that might be more meaningful.

Comparison/Contrast

Comparison questions ask, "What is it similar to, and in what ways is it similar?" Contrast questions ask, "What does it differ from, and in what ways does it differ?" Comparisons and contrasts can serve a variety of functions, each of which may shape the content of your response. Your purpose may be to (a) show differences between typically similar things, (b) show similarities between generally dissimilar things, (c) explain one thing in relation to something else, or (d) serve as a basis for an argument or evaluation. In each case, you might choose to emphasize a different aspect of the information you have on hand.

Comparisons and contrasts can involve a two-step process beginning with definitions and moving to specifying similarities and dissimilarities. Let's say you are asked to "compare and/or contrast Freud's and Skinner's models of moral development." It may be helpful to begin by clearly defining each of the two models. You will find that the very process of defining each lays the groundwork for your subsequent comparison/contrast. After all, you have to know "what it is" before you can discuss what it is like and what it is unlike. On the other hand, definitions alone are rarely sufficient to provide a comparison or contrast. Comparisons and contrasts are asking you to go beyond definitions — to think about the **interrelationship** between characteristics of two or more concepts.

In order to specify the similarities and dissimilarities between the items to be compared and contrasted you need to:

1. **Select the characteristics** which represent the important similarities and dissimilarities between the items to be compared/contrasted. In the case of Freud's and Skinner's models of moral development, these might include (a) importance of parents as role models, (b) historical roots, (c) the role of reinforcement, (d) a definition of morality, etc.

2. **Reorganize** these points into a **logical sequence.** This could mean using a chronological sequence, going from the more general to the more specific characteristics, progressing from those characteristics having the greatest commonalities to those having the least, or whatever makes the most sense for your particular topic. In the case of our example we might choose a combination of the chron-

ological and general-to-specific approaches resulting in the following sequence: (a) historical roots, (b) definition of morality, (c) parents as role models, (d) the role of reinforcement, etc.

3. Explain the similarities and dissimilarities of the concepts, following the logical sequence you planned above. Generally, you begin with the first charcteristic you have planned to discuss (in our example, "historical roots") and explain the similarities and dissimilarities of the models. Then proceed to the second characteristic, the third, and so on, in a similar fashion. In this case, your answer would take this form:

I. Historical Roots
  A. Similarities between Freud's & Skinner's models
  B. Dissimilarities betwen Freud's & Skinner's models
II. Definition of Morality
  A. Similarities between Freud's & Skinner's models
  B. Dissimilarities between Freud's & Skinner's models
III. Parents as Role Models
  A. . . .
  B. . . . and so on

As an alternative, you could begin by discussing *all* of the characteristics of Freud's model according to your planned sequence, then explain the same characteristics of Skinner's model, highlighting the similarities and dissimilarities of each with Freud's. However, this technique is successful only when the comparison or contrast is relatively brief (the reader must remember your first description in order to follow its comparison/contrast with the second).

WRITING 3.4: COMPARISON/CONTRAST. A Human Development exam required students to compare and contrast the major psychosocial characteristics associated with rural and urban influences on the American family. One student, Carl S., used the first half of his answer to consider elements associated with modern, urban settings, and the second half of his response to discuss features that characterize older, rural environments.

The majority of Americans live in a highly

technical, urban society (even the suburbs are becoming urbanized) which to some extent influences behavior. This was not always the case, because it has been only in the last century that the majority of Americans are in urban instead of in rural settings. Now most Americans live in small nuclear families in sharply differentiated neighborhood pockets. Because so many people live close to each other, urban families increasingly tend to live in a state of siege, behind locked and barred doors and windows, with guns and guard dogs.

The urban setting puts special stress on the American nuclear family. Because of the city's fast pace and competitive atmosphere, the family unit has become a haven in a heartless world, the one place where the individual can look for love and forgiveness. On the other hand, even family relationships get affected by the mechanized, special skills required for an urban labor force. Children are brought to day-care centers for the entire day. The children might get to know the day-care workers better than their own parents. At home the children's interactions with their parents are reserved for a couple hours of ''quality time'' somewhere between dinner and bed.

Simpler rural societies tend to integrate the concept of the family into work, play, and household activities. Typically, parents and children work and play side-by-side. The family members share many activities and can talk with each other as they work. Since so many activities in a rural culture are connected to nature and the agrarian life — farming crops, tending livestock, etc. — people tend to develop a relationship to the land and to each other that is relatively uncomplicated and genuine.

Since most rural communities are relatively "closed societies," neighbors share a sense of intimacy and security so that they feel they can leave their doors unlocked at night. Children often see themselves as members of an ''extended family'' that includes not only their blood relatives (who often live

```
nearby if not in the same house) but also their
neighbors (whom the children have known all
their lives).
```

While Carl's generalizations represent a decent start at describing each separate environmental influence, it is also clear that his answer does not present a close comparison/contrast analysis. He has described several important aspects of both the urban and rural worlds, but has not brought the two together as clearly as he might. Use the close point-by-point comparison/contrast structure we describe in this chapter to outline and then draft a rewrite of Carl's analysis (using the information he provided).

Argument/Evaluation

Requests for arguments or evaluations generally ask, "Can you prove it?" You'll find that this is often the ultimate goal of scientific writing. When you approach the process of argument or evaluation, **evidence** is the key ingredient. Your job is to pull together evidence in order to support, contradict, disprove, or perhaps reformulate a claim. So *what exactly constitutes "evidence"*? What's considered evidence by one person may be seen as relatively meaningless trivia by another. That's why it is critical to include a clear statement of the source or basis of the evidence or "data" that you use. Your data may come from published reports of experimentally manipulated research, personal observations, commonly held assumptions, second-hand stories from friends, etc. While all of these may be meaningful sources of information in their own ways, some are seen as more credible and generalizable than others. We'll mention the pros and cons of various sources of information in Chapters 5 and 6. In any case, it is important to specify the source of the data so that readers can form their own opinions about its validity.

When you argue or evaluate a specific premise, where do you begin and how do you proceed? There are at least four major steps:

1. Assemble the evidence. You need to make a list of all the types of "data" that might be relevant to evaluating the issue at hand. Use the exercises described at the end of Chapter 1 to help you start. Don't evaluate it now. Jot down *all* the possibilities. Keep an open mind. If you evaluate your evidence prematurely, you may reject positions which seem "soft" for the moment but which gather considerable support in the long run.

2. Organize the evidence. Now you need to classify the evidence you've assembled, using the strategies of classification discussed earlier. Your goal is to **determine** the various **positions** that are represented by the data you've assembled. Try to think about all the possible ways you could organize or group your data and select the one which gives the most comprehensive and meaningful structure to the evidence. Separating your list of evidence into "pro" versus "con" arguments is an example of a simple classification system. However, you may often find that this is too simplistic for many of the issues you evaluate. There are frequently more than two positions represented within your list of potential evidence. Clustering diagrams (described in Chapter 1) can suggest alternative structures for organization.

3. Evaluate the evidence. Now is the time to examine critically the evidence which supports each of the positions you classified in step 2. A number of factors could be considered here. Perhaps the obvious question to ask is "*how much* evidence do I have for each position?" But the *quantity* of evidence is only one consideration. Equally, if not more important, is the *quality* of information. For example, what is the source of the information supporting each position? As any jury will confirm, reams of data from highly questionable sources are less convincing than a few samples of evidence from very credible sources. Also important may be the *variety* of sources of information supporting each position. Is there *consensus among different sources* in support of a particular position? For example, an argument for personality differences among newborns is more convincing if researchers and parents agree upon this issue than if researchers alone support this position. Similarly, even when all of your evidence arises from a common source (for example, published journal articles), you might ask yourself if the evidence for a particular position comes from a single type of experiment, or whether different research strategies have arrived at the same position. Moreover, you might consider whether any one position is supported by a *variety of investigators*, or simply by multiple works of one particular researcher (or research team). In each case, the issue is the same: The evidence is more convincing if it represents a consensus among different sources, methods, investigators, etc. This consensus makes it less likely that the findings are simply a product of a bias in the approach. We'll return to this point in Chapter 5, when we discuss writing a literature review.

4. Integrate the evidence and take a position. Now that you've evaluated the evidence, it's time to take a stand. This might simply involve selecting the position which appears to have the best support. But, it can involve much more. You can move beyond your earlier classifications of positions to define an entirely new perspective. That is, integrate the evidence to create an original perspective. For example, let's return to the issue of whether or not infants are born with distinct, individual personalities. After assembling, organizing, and evaluating the data, you might conclude that infants are neither born with well-defined, complex personalities nor are they purely a product of their postnatal experiences. Rather, they appear to be born with varying tendencies to adapt or cope with their environments in distinct ways, and their personalities emerge from an interaction of these inborn temperaments and postnatal experiences. It may be that no *single* piece of evidence actually argued for this position, but rather your synthesis of the evidence led you to this perspective.

By now it is probably apparent that argument and evaluation integrate and build upon the forms of writing we discussed earlier: definition, classification, analysis, comparison/contrast. In turn, argument and evaluation may be used to support and develop these individual elements of the essay. In summary, it is crucial to recognize the ways in which these different kinds of information interact and serve one another.

WRITING 3.5: ANALYSIS/ARGUMENT. In the 1960s, Jim Morrison and the rock group The Doors composed a haunting ballad entitled "The End," a song based on a young man who had not resolved his Oedipal yearnings toward his mother and hostility toward his father. In the 1970s, the rock group The Who probed aspects of psychopathology in their rock musicals

"Tommy" and "Quadrophenia." Choose a popular song — rock lyric, musical, sentimental favorite — that you feel embodies a certain set of psychological principles. Write down the lyrics of this song and in a three- to five-page analysis, consider the meaning of the lyrics in relationship to a specific psychological theory you have studied.

TRIAL BY FIRE: WRITING UNDER TIME PRESSURE

We've all felt the anxiety of writing under the pressure of time. Even if you feel as though you've studied sufficiently and rested the night before, staring back and forth from exam to clock can create panic. A common response to this situation is to shift into overdrive and write down everything that comes to mind. Who has the time to consider the writing strategies and techniques we've discussed in this chapter? Although you may need some convincing of this, those strategies are now more important than ever. You don't have the opportunity to ramble on, hoping that by supplying vast amounts of information you'll somehow hit upon the correct answer. When you have limited time and space, it's particularly important that your response is clear and concise. Therefore, in concluding our thoughts on writing essays and examinations, let us offer a few suggestions about writing under time constraints:

1. **Read all the questions before you begin to write.** This can help you distinguish between the kinds of information requested in each, and one question may remind you of material you should cover in another. Decide which essays you intend to discuss and the order in which you'll answer them. (Start with the easiest and work your way to the most difficult. This will help you to gain momentum and confidence.) At this point you should also give yourself time limits for answering each question and don't let yourself exceed those limits. Running out of time is one of the most frequent obstacles to producing a solid exam. Plan some time for reviewing your answers at the end of the exam.

2. **Outline.** Once you decide upon a question, take a couple of minutes to outline your answer. You might just list the key points

to be included in your response and the order in which to present them. In doing so, be sure to address *all* the issues that are raised in the exam question. Remember to ask those preliminary questions we raised at the beginning of this chapter: What kind of information should my answer provide? What form should my answer take? What is the purpose of the question?

3. **Work from the general to the specific.** When writing essays, set up each answer in a "funnel shape": Start broadly, by stating and defining the most important elements of the response. Then, gradually begin to narrow your answer by using more specific examples and illustrations to "flesh out" the points you've established. In this way, your examples will refer to concepts you've explained previously, and your supporting illustrations can be tailored to fit the major points which began your response.

4. **Don't wander.** Provide only that information which is directly relevant to the question. (Here's where your outline can prove particularly helpful.) It may be tempting to try to write down everything you know, hoping you'll hit upon the "right answer." But long, meandering responses suggest imprecise, fuzzy thinking, even when the relevant information is embedded somewhere in your answer. After every few sentences, check yourself: Are you still on course to constructing a relevant response?

5. **Reread and revise.** As we've said, it's best to allocate time to reread and revise your answers when you're planning your writing time at the beginning of the exam. As you review your answers, check for places where a word or phrase might help to make a point more clearly. Save substantial revisions until the end of the exam, when you've finished responding to all of the questions.

WRITING 3.6: A week or two before an exam, write three or four potential essay questions based upon lecture notes and textbook information. Answer at least two of these under exam conditions: Allot the same amount of time your professor intends to allow you. Better yet, do this exercise with a classmate, compare your written answers, and suggest improvements in each.

[4] *Writing to Summarize*

Imagine that you have just spent three hours struggling through a complex article about the effects of adolescent hormonal changes on learning abilities. As you read, you took notes to help yourself decipher the article and remember what it is all about. When you arrive in class, your roommate, who barely made it through the first page of the article, says, "Quick, tell me what the article is about!" And you try. Then your professor enters the class and asks you to take five minutes to jot down the key issues in the article. Finally, as you leave class, you are given the assignment of writing an abstract of the article for your next class meeting.

In each of these instances, you are concerned with summarizing the material from an article. However, in each case the purpose and hence the form and content of the summary is a bit different. In this section we'll briefly discuss how to write article summaries and abstracts, and the way in which this process is shaped by your goals. Later in this chapter, we'll discuss another form of summary, the book and film review. A word of caution: Regardless of how much time and effort you put into composing summaries, abstracts, and reviews, their quality will depend on how thoroughly and accurately you read and understand the original material.

WRITING ARTICLE SUMMARIES AND ABSTRACTS

Let's begin by distinguishing between abstracts and summaries. In general terms, an abstract is simply a summary. However, the term *abstract* has taken on a special meaning in psychology (and in many other social and natural sciences as well). Its special meaning emerges from the fact that the psychological abstract has formal requirements in both content and form which have been standardized virtually worldwide. An abstract is formal and impersonal; its format and length are prescribed by the conventions of the discipline. On the other hand, a general summary of a paper or book may be formal or informal, objective or personalized; its form, content, and length will vary to suit the writer's needs. Let's briefly consider summaries. Then we'll focus in more detail on abstracts.

Summaries

As we've said, a summary is personal, idiosyncratic. It has no formal guidelines. Rather, its form and content will be determined by its intended purpose, subject, and audience. In the example at the beginning of this section, we mentioned several possible reasons for summarizing an article. You might write a summary in your journal in order to help you clarify your thinking about the article. In this case, your summary might or might not be comprehensive; it might or might not be detailed. Moreover, it might or might not be written in a way that could be understood by an outside reader. The summary might meander back and forth between your personal experience and only one of the paper's many themes. Or it might compare this and another article's perspective on one relatively small but controversial issue. On the other hand, you may have summarized an article in reviewing for an exam. In this case you'd probably want to be more comprehensive and include all those key points made in the article.

The summary of the article which you provide for your roommate is likely to be very different. Your goal here is to communicate a general overview of the information to an individual who is relatively unfamiliar with the material. This summary needs to teach another person new information rather than remind you of connections you have already considered. So, while less comprehensive than your summary for exam preparation, it must be relatively detailed.

Your five-minute class exercise in jotting down the article's key issues is unique in yet other ways. Your goal is to evaluate, that is, to rank the significance of the issues raised. You must be comprehensive in pointing to each of the key issues, but you need not be particularly detailed on any. You assume that the audience (the professor and/or you) is somewhat versed in the area, so your intent is to integrate and identify issues rather than to reiterate details or teach the information to a naive reader.

Because summaries can serve so many different functions, it is important to identify your goals before writing. The most efficient and effective summary writing is highly sensitive to its intended purpose, audience, and subject matter. While any one summary may be brilliant in meeting one set of goals, it may be a disaster in terms of achieving another.

WRITING 4.1: SUMMARIES. Select an article which you have been assigned to read for a psychology course. After carefully reading it, write a one-page summary of the article. Before you begin, be certain to specify your purpose and audience, then compose your summary accordingly.

Abstracts

The main purpose of an abstract is to provide a concise but comprehensive summary of an article or book which will allow readers to decide whether the full text is of interest to them. Abstracts are used in two contexts: (1) They are usually the first section of any journal article, whether it be a theoretical/review article or a report of empirical research. (2) They are used in indexing or information services (e.g., *Psychological Abstracts*), where they are organized by date, subject matter, etc., to allow people to search systematically for information of interest. As the *Publication Manual of the American Psychological Association* suggests, "A well-prepared abstract can be the single most important paragraph in the article. An abstract (a) is read first, (b) may be the only part of an article that is actually read (readers frequently decide, on the basis of the abstract, whether to read the entire article), and (c) is an important means of access in locating and retrieving the article" (American Psychological Association, 1983, p. 23).

Does this mean that you need to worry about how to write abstracts only if you are at the point of writing journal articles? Definitely not! In addition to its formal purpose of providing information for the reader, composing an abstract serves an important function for you, the writer: It leads you to analyze and identify carefully the real essence of the material you're covering. Perhaps you are to abstract a library article which you've just spent two hours reading. Or maybe you are to abstract a research project in which you've assisted for the last couple of years. In both cases, writing an abstract requires that you wade through a tremendous amount of information and pull together a very concise but comprehensive description of its core. The significance of this process will become clear in the following discussion of the specific form and content requirements of a formal abstract.

The requirements of an abstract vary depending upon whether you're abstracting an empirical research report or a review or theoretical article. An **empirical research report** discusses original research which has been conducted by the author(s). In your psychology classes, this is what is typically referred to as a lab report or simply a research report (see Chapter 7). A **review article** pulls together material which has already been published, integrating and often evaluating the existing knowledge on the topic. In your psychology classes, this is what is often referred to as a literature review (see Chapter 5). **Theoretical articles** are written to advance theory in the field, by critiquing or refining existing theory, and/or presenting a new theoretical perspective. Theoretical articles refer to original or existing empirical work only insofar as it specifically affects theoretical issues. Now consider the requirements of an abstract for each.

Empirical Research Report

An abstract for an **empirical research report** can be only 100–150 words long — even if the work took five years to complete and/or the article was twenty-five pages long. The abstract is typed as a single paragraph in block format (i.e., without paragraph indentation at its beginning). According to the American Psychological Association (APA, 1983, p. 24), it should include the following:

1. a statement of the problem investigated (perhaps including the hypothesis tested) ideally in no more than one sentence;
2. the subjects of the study, including their relevant characteristics, such as number, age, sex, and species;
3. the research procedure, including any special apparatus and tests or assessments, and data gathering techniques, as specific as necessary (within space constraints) in order to represent their importance in the experiment;
4. the main results of the study;
5. the conclusions and implications (or even applications) of the study.

Here is an example of a student's abstract of an empirical report:

Effects of Labeling and Handicap Appearance on
Peers' First Impressions

by Eden Stein
University of Vermont

Abstract

This study investigated the interactive effects of labeling and handicap appearance of exceptional children on the attitudes of their peers. Sixty third-graders saw photographs of non-handicapped, Down's Syndrome, and physically handicapped children, with half of the stimuli labeled "handicapped," in a $2 \times 2 \times 3$ factorial design (Label × Sex × Handicap). Peers' attitudes were measured in terms of perceived attractiveness, behavioral intentions, and an adjective checklist of personality traits. Ratings of attractiveness and attitudes varied as a function of labeling and sex; girls' reports were positively affected by labeling, while boys' were negatively affected. The effect of labeling also varied with handicap, negatively affecting attitudes toward children with no obvious handicap but enhancing impressions of those with an

```
obvious physical handicap. These findings need be
considered in light of the effect of first impres-
sions upon subsequent impression formation.
```

WRITING 4.2: ABSTRACTS. Reread the sample abstract above and mark the words or sentences which address each of the five items required in an abstract of an empirical report.

Review or Theoretical Article

An abstract of a **review article** or of a **theoretical article** is quite similar to that of an empirical report but a bit shorter, 75–100 words. Again, it is to be typed as a single paragraph in block format (no paragraph indentation). According to the American Psychological Association (APA, 1983, p. 24), its contents should include:

1. a brief statement of the topic (one sentence);
2. an indication of the paper's position or purpose as well as its scope (i.e., whether it is comprehensive or selective);
3. a mention of the types of sources that the article used (e.g., published literature, personal observation, etc.);
4. the conclusions and implications or applications of the article.

Here is an example of a published abstract of a review article (Freedman, 1984, p. 227):

Effect of Television Violence on Aggressiveness

JONATHAN L. FREEDMAN
University of Toronto, Ontario, Canada

This article reviews the available field and correlational research on the effects of viewing television violence on subsequent aggressiveness. The work is described and criticized, and the findings are assessed. Two conclusions are reached: First, there is a consistent, small positive correlation between viewing television violence and aggressiveness; second, there is little convincing evidence that in natural settings viewing television violence causes people to be more aggressive. The significance of these conclusions and possible explanations are discussed.

WRITING 4.3: Reread the sample abstract on television violence. Mark which words or sentences address each of the four items required in an abstract of a review article.

Characteristics of a Good Abstract

As you can see, the abstract, while very brief, must also be comprehensive, and that's where the difficulty arises. How can you put all that information in just 75–150 words (⅓–½ a typed page)? It definitely is not easy. That's why writing an abstract is an excellent means for distilling, communicating, and preserving the essence of an article or project. Writing an abstract, whether based on your own or another's research, serves to crystallize your understanding and appreciation of the basic elements of a scholarly work.

The American Psychological Association (APA, 1983) makes several suggestions worth keeping in mind. A good abstract is:

1. Accurate. The abstract must accurately reflect the paper. Not only should you avoid actual errors in representing the article, but you should also avoid over- or understating its emphasis on various points or procedures. There shouldn't be any information in the abstract which was not originally in the paper (e.g., your own interpretations).

2. Concise and specific. Each sentence should pack as much information as possible and, at the same time, be brief. Imagine that each word you use costs you $1; are you sure you really need to include it? In order to be as concise as possible, you'll also need to use very specific words; you don't have space to elaborate. Consider the following portion of an abstract:

a. The present study examined the hypothesis that children's memory abilities are positively related to general intelligence. The subjects of the study were forty children who were in first grade. All of them were males. Each subject was administered a Stanford Binet Intelligence test while seated alone with a trained tester. The tester was always a male. Each subject then completed a free recall task in which items to be recalled were members of the same category. . . .

Not bad, is it? It seems fairly brief and to the point. This portion of the abstract, however, is seventy-seven words long (3/4 of the allotted length), and it has not yet begun to mention the results and conclusions. Now spend a few minutes editing the example above. Are there ways you can condense it without losing information? Look for repetition. Are there unnecessary words? Where would you make changes if this were your abstract?

In fact, a number of the words are unnecessary or redundant. This becomes clear if you think about making a telegraph out of your draft:

> ~~The present study~~ examined ~~the hypothesis that~~ children's memory abilities are positively related to general intelligence. ~~The subjects of the study were~~ forty ~~children who were in~~ first grade. ~~All of them were~~ males. ~~Each~~ subject was administered a Stanford Binet intelligence test ~~while seated~~ alone ~~with a~~ trained tester. ~~The tester was always a~~ male. ~~Each subject then completed a~~ free recall task ~~in which~~ items ~~to be recalled were members of the~~ same category. . . .

When this telegraph is then rewritten into complete sentences you've got the following revision:

> b. To examine whether children's memory abilities and general intelligence are positively related, forty male first graders were individually administered the Stanford Binet Intelligence test and a free recall task of categorized items by a trained male tester. . . .

We've reduced the material to only thirty-seven words (less than half the original), and seem to have retained all the information. You shouldn't expect to write your first draft in such a brief and concise form. In fact, example (a), above, would serve as a very nice first draft. Just start by getting down all the essential information, then revise until you've achieved your goal.

3. **Self-contained.** Your abstract should be able to stand on its own; the reader should not have to refer to the original paper to understand it. This means that you should define abbreviations, acronyms, and highly unique terms, and spell out the names of un-

common tests or drugs. Also, paraphrase rather than quote.

4. Nonevaluative. Simply report what's in the paper. Don't add judgements or evaluations of your own. Nothing belongs in the abstract that's not in the original text. Therefore, when you note the purpose of the study in the abstract, state the purpose as it is stated in the original paper. Similarly, when you comment upon the conclusions and implications of the paper, summarize those that are outlined in the full paper. The abstract is not the place to add your own thoughts and creative insights.

5. Coherent and readable. Use clear prose and active verbs rather than passive voice (e.g., "analyses revealed" rather than "it was revealed by the analyses"). You'll find this is usually more concise. Use the past tense to refer to procedures that were used or variables that were manipulated in the study (e.g., "subjects completed a paired-associate learning task," "drug dosage equalled .01% of animal weight"). Use present tense to refer to results that have continuing application and to conclusions which are drawn (e.g., "these findings support the theory that . . . ," "it appears that memory is positively related to intelligence").

We've discussed the form, content, and characteristics of a good abstract. Here are some suggestions for putting it all together:

1. Recall the items of content necessary for a complete abstract.

For an empirical report

1. the problem
2. the subjects
3. the procedure
4. the results
5. the conclusions, implications

For a theoretical or review article

1. the topic
2. the thesis and scope
3. the sources used
4. the conclusions, implications

Select the list of items which is appropriate for the article you're abstracting and write just a few words or a brief statement about each point. Don't worry about making complete sentences; in fact, you probably don't even want to use sentences yet. For now, your goal is to get all the essential information down on paper. Continually refer to the original paper to be sure that you're being accurate and that you're neither over- or understating issues nor adding information to the original article.

2. Review the list of information you've compiled and decide whether each point is *truly* essential. An abstract is just a summary; it can't say everything. It's intended to *represent* rather than *fully describe* the article (remember the telegraph).

3. Now transform the information into a coherent and readable form. Using clear, concise prose; try to express the abstracted information in a logical series of complete sentences. Your statements should generally follow the sequence we used when listing the items of content above. Write this draft of your abstract in the single paragraph block format. Now, count the number of words you've got to see how you're doing.

4. Revise your draft, attempting to be more concise and specific. As we demonstrated in the example above, you can often cut the length of your abstract in half without losing any information. You'll probably need to repeat this step several times. If you get stuck and feel there is simply no way to condense your abstract further, ask a friend to read it. Or put the abstract aside and return to it later. You'll be surprised how many "essential" words become quite unessential then.

5. Once you feel you've got a polished product, review the characteristics of a good abstract. Is your abstract an accurate representation of the article? Is it self-contained and therefore fully understandable on its own? Is it nonevaluative, reporting only what is included in the original article? Is it concise and specific? Is it readable and coherent? If the answer to all of these questions is yes, the odds are you've created a good abstract.

WRITING 4.4: ABSTRACTS. Following the guidelines above, write an abstract for the article which you summarized in Writing 4.1. If the article already includes an abstract, don't reexamine it until you have completed your own abstract. Then compare the two. What are the strengths and weaknesses of each?

COMPOSING BOOK AND FILM REVIEWS

In high school you were probably asked to write book reports. Most likely, they consisted of a plot summary: You retold the major points of the book and perhaps mentioned what you liked most about reading it. A book or film review for your psychology class requires you to do more.

There are two distinct types of book/film reviews in psychology. One is a **review of a psychology book or film**; the other is a **psychological analysis of a popular book or film.** While the former typically considers a scholarly work in the field (for example, Domjan & Burkhard's, 1986, *The Principles of Learning & Behavior*) the latter may consider a novel, a biography, or even Saturday morning cartoons. These two types of reviews differ in purpose, content, and audience. We'll consider each in turn.

Book/Film Review I: A Review of a Psychology Book or Film

Reviews of psychology books and films serve several functions for the professional psychologist and the student. First, no one has time to read or view everything. By reading a brief review we might be able to decide if it is worthwhile for us to read the entire book or see the entire film. Does it deal with the content we want, the orientation we're interested in? Is it well written, well documented, convincing? A good review should answer these questions for us. Reading reviews of psychology books and films also allows us to keep track of what's happening in our field and related fields. Are there new directions of thinking which may be important in shaping the ways in which we think about our own work? Again, a good review can fill us in.

You may have seen reviews in certain magazines such as the *Atlantic* or *Harper's*, or in book review journals like the *New York Times Book Review*. Perhaps the best source of psychology book reviews is the journal *Contemporary Psychology;* it is devoted entirely to reviews of recently published books in psychology. Here is an example (from *Contemporary Psychology*, 1984, 29, p. 906).

Operant Learning in Physical Rehabilitation

Elaine Greif and Ruth G. Matarazzo. **Behavioral Approaches to Rehabilitation: Coping With Change. Springer Series on Rehabilitation, Vol. 3.** New York: Springer Publishing, 1982. 171 pp. $16.95 cloth; $13.95 paper

Review by GEOFFREY L. THORPE

Elaine Greif is a psychologist in the Department of Health Care Psychology at Emanuel Hospital in Portland, Oregon. ■ *Ruth G. Matarazzo is professor of medical psychology at the Oregon Health Sciences University. She contributed the chapter "Research on the Teaching and Learning of Psychotherapeutic Skills" to S. L. Garfield and A. E. Bergin's* Handbook of Psychotherapy and Behavior Change. ■ *Geoffrey L. Thorpe is associate professor in the Department of Psychology at the University of Maine at Orono. He is coauthor of* The Agoraphobic Syndrome: Behavioural Approaches to Evaluation and Treatment *with L. E. Burns.*

This book is intended to serve as a practical handbook for caregivers in a physical rehabilitation setting. The authors give illuminating descriptions of everyday issues that arise in rehabilitation and suggest appropriate psychosocial treatment interventions. Most of the suggested interventions are applications of behavior change principles derived from operant learning theory. The authors call attention to the ubiquity of behavioral contingencies, whether arranged deliberately or not. The abundant case illustrations are very helpful here. For example, a staff member who sometimes accedes to unreasonable requests by a patient, or to demands presented in an inappropriate way, risks strengthening those very behaviors by means of intermittent social reinforcement. It is more effective for the staff member to offer help sometimes when it is not requested, as well as to respond to appropriate requests, so that inadvertent and unhelpful reinforcement contingencies are not established.

The authors begin the book by defining rehabilitation as a multifaceted effort in which professionals and programs lay the foundation for the real work — which is accomplished by the patient at home in the community. They then describe the typical stages through which people pass in their attempts to cope with disability. After a simplified account of operant learning, the authors present a series of chapters on the management of specific problem behavior patterns — depression, anxiety, disorientation, and so on. It is clear from these chapters that the intended readership is paraprofessional. For example, caregivers are advised to help depressed patients by listening to their concerns, encouraging graded activities, and if necessary, referring them to specialists for counseling or for medication. There is a section on coping skills for caretakers, and the book ends with an illustrative case history and a series of appendixes on treatment aids and resources.

The authors write economically and plainly. They avoid using sexist language by alternating case examples of males with those of females. The rich variety of clinical illustrations attests to the authors' experience, expertise, and enthusiasm. The discussion sometimes hints at a controlling style: "Schedules avoid the necessity for repeated bargaining and decision making where the patient may choose to agree or disagree with the proposed program. Routines build habits that are resistant to the influence of changing moods" (p. 58). Throughout the book, however, the authors emphasize respect for the patient and eloquently oppose demeaning interactions: "Too often, elderly patients are spoken to as if they were children . . . lose privacy over their bodies and immediate space . . . and see decisions being made for them without their consultation" (p. 88).

Understandably enough, there is little here for the theoretically oriented psychologist, who would find the outline of principles shallow. The authors use the technical term *reinforcement,* but sometimes equate it with reward rather than with the strengthening or encouragement of specific behaviors; this inconsistency makes one wonder whether it might have been better to omit the technical term altogether. Consulting psychologists will find in the book a concise summary of important psychosocial issues in rehabilitation and will probably want to have it on hand to recommend to direct-care staff as a training resource.

Professors might ask you to write a review of a psychology book or film because they want to help you develop analytical skills, to give you practice in presenting main ideas and supporting them with a line of reasoning, and to encourage you to make critical assessments of psychology sources. Also, writing a review of a scholarly psychology book exposes you to primary literature.

While the specifics of the assignment may vary from class to class, a good review of a psychology book should meet these goals:

1. Identify the book completely: author or editor, full title, publisher, and place and date of publication.
2. Describe the subject and scope of the book.

3. Give information about the author, focusing on his or her qualifications for writing this book. (Ask the reference librarian for help in finding this information.)
4. Outline or summarize the thrust or argument of the book, giving the main pieces of evidence to support the author's position.
5. Tell whether the author, in your judgement, satisfactorily supports the thesis or argument.
6. Connect the book to the larger world by explaining the ramifications of the argument or material, assessing the value of the book, or placing it in the context of public issues or of other current books on the subject.
7. Relate the book's subject or thesis to the academic course.

WRITING 4.5: READING A PSYCHOLOGY BOOK REVIEW. If you haven't already done so, read the book review above, "Operant Learning in Physical Rehabilitation." As you read, look for the elements of a good book review explained above and mark them in the margins. For instance, mark with a "2" the paragraph or sentence where the review describes the subject and scope of the book. Are any of the elements listed above omitted? Can you think of reasons for the omission? Which of the elements receive the most extensive treatment? Can you suggest why? This exercise should give you a better idea of one individual's approach to reviewing a psychology book.

WRITING 4.6: WRITING A PSYCHOLOGY BOOK REVIEW. Choose a recent book within the scope of your psychology course (your professor may provide a list of titles or suggest that you look for a list of recommended books in your text). Before you read the book, review the guidelines given earlier. Knowing what you're looking for will help you read more efficiently. When you write your review, refer to the guidelines frequently, but don't feel enslaved. Let your own responses to the book show through.

Book/Film Review II: A Psychological Analysis of a Book or Film

We often use psychological jargon in our daily conversations when we're trying to describe or explain a friend's behavior. Much of psychology can be applied to our everyday behaviors and experiences. Therefore, you shouldn't be surprised if your professor asks you to write a psychological analysis or review of a popular novel or film.

It may be important to use some plot summary in this sort of review; however, a plot summary is not what's most important. Instead, the emphasis of this review is to analyze major elements of a book or film in connection with specific concepts learned in your psychology class. In other words, you are less interested in retelling what happened in the film or novel, and more concerned with analyzing relationships between *selective* scenes and/or themes and *specific* psychological principles.

Here are excerpts from two students' film reviews of *Ordinary People*. This is a film about the personal and interpersonal struggles of an adolescent named Conrad and his family, several years after the boating accident death of Conrad's older brother, Buck. Even if you haven't seen the film, these excerpts should provide examples of what works and what doesn't work in a review.

Each has set out to analyze Conrad's psychological state. Notice that the first student approaches the task by focusing on a general analysis of the plot's overall theme.

> Conrad distorts whatever happens around him as his responsibility (i.e., Buck's death). Conrad has an extremely negative self-image, even though most of his life he has been very successful and competitive. In fact, it may be the high standards that Conrad set up for himself which lead to his failure. He set standards so high (his model was Buck, and if his ideal could not survive then he should not have been able to either) that failure was inevitable and unforgivable. Once he messed up he began to interpret his world in a way that made him ultimately responsible. He tried to take on Buck's role but could not do it, so he sees that as a deficit in his abilities (once more making him feel

guilty and inadequate). Rather than realizing he was a different person separate from Buck, he saw himself as a failure because he could not become Buck.

While this passage states the basic themes of *Ordinary People* and outlines Conrad's general state of mind, it fails to consider the relationship among these elements and specific psychological theory. The student records Conrad's general feelings without attempting to analyze these emotions in terms of particular psychological principles. For instance, it may be true that Conrad struggles to "take on Buck's role," but the writer never provides examples of this nor indicates how this type of behavior could be explained in concrete psychological terms. In other words, the review fails to provide a specific psychological theory or framework for understanding Conrad's life.

In contrast, consider this excerpt from another student's review:

Beck's cognitive theory of depression hypothesizes that psychological dysfunctions are the result of the way people think about themselves, their world, and the future. Depressed people typically exhibit characteristic self-defeating thoughts or cognitive distortions. They view themselves as inadequate and systematically misinterpret events in their lives to confirm their negative self-image. What happens in many cases is that depressed individuals won't exhibit the negative schema until an unfortunate or distressing life event occurs which brings the negative schema out of its dormant state. In Conrad's case, he developed a negative schema early on by constantly being confronted by Buck and his success. He developed a view of himself that made him feel inferior to Buck. This did not make Conrad maladaptive when Buck was living because Conrad shared in Buck's success and Conrad also received approval from his parents. However, when Buck died, the negative schema became maladaptive because it was Conrad who survived, proving himself superior in this instance. This traumatic event activated the negative schema and made it more prominent in his behavior and thought, thus resulting in depres-

> sion. This fits in with Ellis' ABC model (Ellis, as cited in Kendall & Norton-Ford, 1982), where "A," the activating event, was Buck's death and "C," the consequences, were that Conrad became depressed due to "B," his beliefs he held in regard to the relationship with his brother.

While the grammar and sentence structure are far from perfect, this student's review successfully provides a context for understanding Conrad's behavior and state of mind — a cognitive theory of depression (the detailed references to Beck and Ellis). The student has connected specific principles of this psychological perspective with particular aspects of Conrad's life. This integration of psychological theory with the film's plot provides a more profound understanding of Conrad's personal crisis. (This is not to say that a cognitive perspective is necessarily the only or even the best interpretation, but the review successfully establishes it as a possibility.) It's also important to note the way this second review moves from the general to the specific: First it describes how human depression characteristically manifests itself, and then it illustrates its points with examples of Conrad's behavior. This approach shows a writer who is in control of the information and an analysis that is both persuasive and comprehensive.

With the above examples in mind, here is a summary of guidelines to use when writing this sort of psychological analysis or review of a book or film for a psychology course:

1. Do not retell the tale. Rather than attempt a complete plot synopsis, narrow your analysis to one or two main aspects which can be traced through a major portion of the plot. Define the significance of your focus and examine only those issues which add insight to it. Make sure the aspect(s) you choose is related to a psychological theory, principle, or assumption. Don't feel you must cover all aspects of a novel or film just because you are reviewing it. For example, if you are reviewing the film *One Flew Over the Cuckoo's Nest* for an abnormal psychology course, a review on all the mental disorders evidenced in this movie would be too broad and could not be analyzed in a short essay. Perhaps a better topic would be an examination of the mental facility itself and the attitude of the attendants toward institutionalized people. Or you might focus specifically upon the effects of labeling individuals "mentally ill," or upon the dehumanizing conditions of institutions.

2. Discriminate among scenes. Once you have sufficiently defined and narrowed your topic, focus upon a few representative scenes which illustrate your thesis. Remember that even in a review you are using the techniques of persuasion or argumentation — trying to convince your reader of the accuracy of your interpretation. Therefore, you must provide evidence to support your thinking. Be thorough in your examination, and be sure to tie the scenes' events closely to the theme of your review.

3. Integrate your own perspective into the review. Keep in mind throughout your review that you are composing it for a psychology course. Consequently, you should carefully consider the validity of the theoretical assumptions that are made in the text. Compare and/or contrast your knowledge of the issue being discussed with the text's representation of it. To return to our earlier illustration, does *One Flew Over the Cuckoo's Nest* pose a convincing critique of patient/staff relationships in mental institutions? Why or why not? Is the movie's perspective on this issue a fair or balanced representation? To address these and related questions, you must combine the movie's attitude toward your topic with your own knowledge of the area. Furthermore, evaluate the significance of the text in terms of its value to the body of knowledge in psychology. What new insights does the film or book contribute to the profession's understanding of that topic?

WRITING 4.7: COMPOSING BOOK AND FILM REVIEWS. Incorporating the writing strategies we have just outlined, select a book you have read recently or a film you have seen recently and write a three- to five-page review. Almost any book or movie will do, as long as it concerns people (and even those that don't might be appropriate). It needn't have been explicitly psychological in focus. It is your task to establish relationships between the content of the movie or book and specific psychological principles you have covered in your class.

[5] *The Literature Review*

PREVIEW:

A newly divorced father struggles with the question of care for his preschoolers. He wonders, "Should I quit my job so that I can be a full-time parent? Should I work nights so that I can be home with the kids during the day? How would the kids adjust to being cared for by a new person?"

The six week maternity leave has ended and a new mom grapples with whether or not she'll go back to work. She debates, "How would it feel to be away from my baby at this point? Would leaving my career harm my sense of competence, even as a parent? How will my decision affect my child's development?"

A congressional subcommittee attempts to formulate recommendations for federally mandated services for children. The members ask, "Should we create programs which encourage parents to stay home with their preschoolers rather than to work? Should we support small, private, family day care homes or large, public, day care centers?"

This is just a sample of current questions relevant to the issue of day care. How do the experts find solutions to these questions? Rather than rely on intuition, common sense, or one particular study, they consult a comprehensive **literature review** of the area.

THE LITERATURE REVIEW: WHAT IS IT AND WHY BOTHER?

The literature review is a comprehensive summary of the research (and/or sometimes theory) on a specific topic. As you'll see, however, it involves much more than simply describing one published article after another. A good review entails **analysis** and **integration** of the literature. It not only gathers relevant information physically into one place, but it also pulls together the information *conceptually.* Therefore, the literature review is one of the mainstays of disseminating as well as generating knowledge in psychology (and most social and natural sciences). Not only does the review say, "Here's what is currently known," but a good review also says, "Here's where we need to go."

Psychology is an **empirical** discipline; that is, it is based on experiment and observation. Moreover, psychology is intended to be a **predictive** science, moving from understanding to anticipating behavior in new situations. In turn, psychological knowledge is **cumulative.** Any single study can offer us little conclusive information; it is the accumulation of findings that gives us direction in understanding and predicting. Empirical, predictive, and cumulative — it is the literature review which allows us to achieve these aims.

Consequently, the literature review can be helpful in a variety of ways to psychologists, students, policy makers, and interested laypersons. Light and Pillemer (1984) identify four major purposes which literature reviews serve:

1. "Well-done reviews can identify general trends that are unlikely to emerge in any single study, however broad or well designed" (p. 144). An illustration of this point is Kilmer's (1979) review of the effects of infant/toddler group day care on child development. Over one hundred studies have examined the issue. Not surprisingly, each asked the question somewhat differently. Some looked at infant day care, some at preschool programs. Some looked at home-based programs, others at center-based programs. Some studied day care's effect on social development, others examined its effect on cognitive development. Some assessed cognitive development in terms of IQ, others measured it in terms of problem-solving ability, and so on. Each of these variations influenced the conclusions. Kilmer assembled the numerous studies on the topic and organized them according to the types of day care effects examined — effects on mother/child relationships, the child's social relationships with persons other than the mother, the child's cognitive development, and the child's physical health. After reviewing the literature and the discrepancies within it, Kilmer drew conclusions about the general trends in each of these areas. Thus, whereas any *one* study can only give us information based upon the specific combination of circumstances or variables it has studied, a good review of the general literature can give us a broader understanding of major trends in the area.

2. "Reviews help to interpret other findings: Some reviews give general insight into interpreting research studies" (Light & Pillemer, 1984, p. 147). As an illustration, Light and Pillemer point to Rosenthal and Rubin's (1982) review of gender differences in cognitive abilities. By reviewing many studies, Rosenthal and Rubin concluded that males typically have outperformed females on most cognitive tasks (except tasks of verbal ability). However, the authors revealed that the degree to which gender differences were found was related to the publication date of the research. Even within the past few decades, the more recent the study, the less the gender difference in performance. This insight is tremendously important, given the debate about whether gender differences in performance result mainly from genetic or environmental factors.

3. "Reviews can resolve controversies . . . they can systematically examine the impact of different research designs or different treatment formats. This can sometimes help to resolve apparent

conflicts in a research literature" (Light & Pillemer, 1984, p. 149). For example, social support has been found to be positively related to psychological well-being. However, there has been controversy about whether this relationship is due to direct benefits of social support (i.e., social support, itself, makes you feel better) or indirect effects (i.e., social support protects you from experiencing stressful events — the buffering model) (Cohen & Wills, 1985). Cohen and Wills reviewed a large number of studies which have examined stress and social support. They concluded that whether research supported one model or the other depended upon the way the study measured social support. The buffering model was confirmed when social support was measured in terms of "perceived availability of interpersonal resources" relevant to stressful events. Evidence for a direct effect was found when social support was defined in terms of the degree to which a person was integrated in a large social network. The authors concluded that "each represents a different process through which social support may affect well-being" (Cohen & Wills, 1984, p. 310).

4. "Reviews can teach broad lessons about accumulating evidence" (Light & Pillemer, 1984, p. 153). These lessons include the facts that most individual studies find small effects, and it's the degree of consistency across studies that determines how meaningful the findings are; the same question will lead to different answers if different research designs are employed, and reviews can reveal interactions between variables which, themselves, were not specifically examined in any given study. The first two of these points were illustrated in the earlier examples. The third point can best be seen in a recent student literature review. In her explorations into the relationship between empathy and aggressive behavior, this student discovered that research which involved children under five or six years old found high levels of interpersonal conflict associated with high levels of empathy. However, studies of children seven or more years old found the reverse: High levels of conflict were associated with low levels of empathy. Therefore, she was able to conclude that the relationship between social aggression and empathy varies with the age of the subject.

In summary, literature reviews serve as a basis for not only answering questions, but also for redefining and raising important questions. In doing so, they can help to guide our research, our policy decisions, and our day-to-day behavior. Now let us consider the steps involved in composing a literature review.

PREWRITING THE LITERATURE REVIEW

When undertaking a literature review, most of the time and effort is spent in the prewriting stage: choosing a topic, finding sources in the literature, reading and taking notes, defining the purpose, audience, and voice, and analyzing and organizing the material. Don't skimp on any of these tasks. Regardless of how good a writer you are, adequate preparation at the prewriting stage is essential for a solid literature review — this is what determines the substance of your paper.

Choosing a Subject

Sometimes an instructor will assign a specific subject or present you with a list of subjects from which to choose. But often you are left to your own devices to find one. Although choosing a paper topic often seems to involve a totally unstructured process and results in an arbitrary decision, it shouldn't. There are certain steps you can take to make the selection process less overwhelming and more productive.

Turn to your journal. If you've been making regular entries in a journal, it's likely to be a rich source of paper topics. What class topics sparked questions in your mind? Which were issues that seemed controversial? What daily observations or experiences seemed particularly relevant to the course? Where did you disagree with the authors of your readings? Were there issues you returned to again and again in your entries? Which journal entries were most interesting to write? These are all sources of a potentially important and thought-provoking topic. Pay attention to other informal writing sources as well — billboards, grafitti, personal ads, etc. can get you wondering, and *wondering* often signals a good topic.

Browse through your textbooks. The texts assigned for your course are likely to present a broad and current overview of the field. Although you may need to select a paper topic early in the semester, before you've read much of your text, browse ahead to get a sense of key issues in the field.

Skim abstracts and professional journals. When you're unfamiliar with a field, it's often difficult to understand the kinds of questions or issues it considers. It can be helpful to spend an hour or two in the library skimming relevant journals or abstracts (see Chapter 8). Select a journal which focuses specifically on your course material (your instructor can help you identify one) or find the section in the *Psychological Abstracts* which deals with the general content of your course.

WRITING 5.1: CHOOSING A GENERAL SUBJECT AREA. Generate four possible subject areas for an eight- to twelve-page literature review. Get at least one from your journal, one from your textbooks, and one from skimming abstracts or professional journals. Make a journal entry in which you summarize what you know already and what you'd like to know about each topic.

Determining the Scope of Your Paper

How broadly or narrowly should you define your topic? The scope of your topic will be shaped, in part, by the purpose of your review. But a general guideline is that you should define it narrowly enough so that you can read nearly every source that has directly addressed the topic. At the same time, your topic should be broad enough so that there are a substantial number of high-quality sources for you to review. A particular number of references may be specified by your instructor; you should usually have ten or more references for an integrative review.

Once you arrive at a general subject area for your paper, there are several techniques you can use to narrow or broaden its focus. In Chapter 1 we discussed a technique called **clustering** which allows you to discover the individual elements of a subject and the relationships among those elements. Defining the scope of your literature review presents an excellent opportunity to use clustering. If you need to narrow your topic, first write down your general subject and circle it. This will be the hub of your cluster. Surround it with the major subdivisions (or related aspects) of the topic; circle each of these and connect each to the main topic with a line. Repeat the process using each subdivision as the hub of another constellation of further divisions or details. Continue to repeat this procedure until you've established a group of manageable topics. Figure 5.1 is an example of a student's clustering of ideas for a paper on aspects of memory strategies. She ended up writing her paper on training programs for the use of memory strategies.

If you need to broaden your topic, the process is essentially the

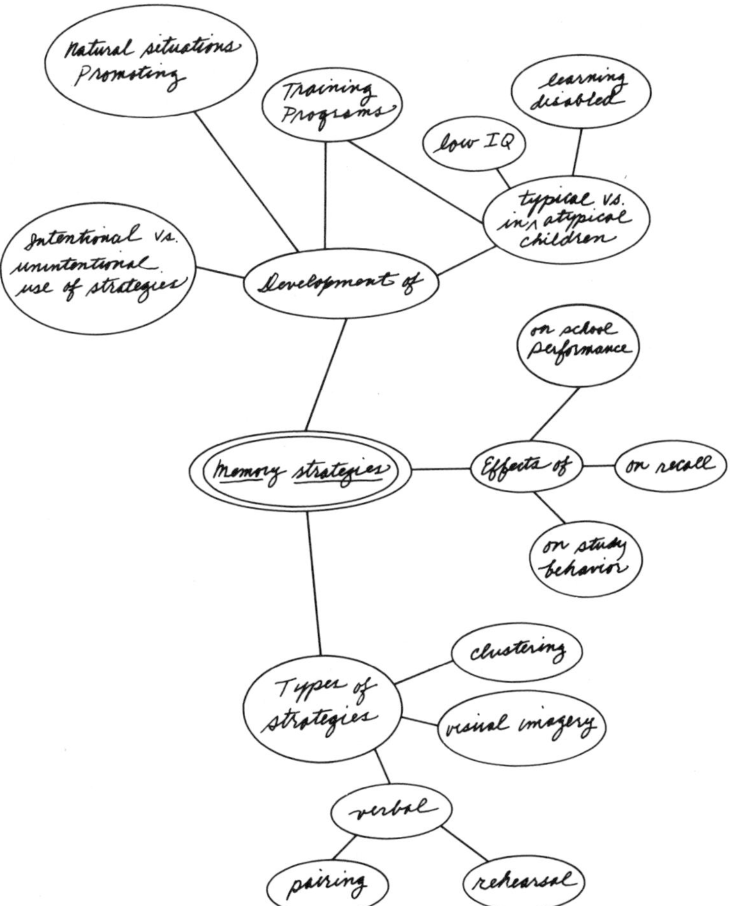

Figure 5.1 *Clustering*

same, but you can work in the reverse direction. Using the example above, the student might have begun the process sparked by an interest in the memory strategies of learning-disabled individuals and then broadened the topic to training programs.

While selecting your topic, follow these few guidelines: (1) Start early — choosing a topic always takes more time than you expect, and you may require considerable redefining of your topic as you go. (2) Select a topic which *you* find interesting; if it doesn't interest you, it will be difficult to make it interesting to your reader. Moreover, you're going to spend a lot of time working with the subject. It'll be more rewarding if you care about the topic. (3) Don't define your topic too broadly or too narrowly — this is a common mistake of student writers. If your topic is too broad, you'll be forced to cover the area superficially. If your topic is too narrow, you won't have much to review or integrate.

WRITING 5.2: DETERMINING THE SCOPE OF YOUR TOPIC. Decide which two or three of the subjects you generated in Writing 5.1 are most interesting to you. Use the clustering technique to explore elements of each of these topics. Based on your clusters, make a list of three possible topics that seem appropriate in scope.

Previewing the Literature

Before committing yourself to a particular topic, it is essential to preview the literature, that is, to determine what sources are available on your subject. Chapter 8 details the procedures for finding resources in the library. Don't forget to use more obvious sources as well, such as your textbooks and references listed in articles and books you have found. However, remember that only a *systematic* library search will assure that you have covered your topic thoroughly.

It's best to begin previewing the literature with a few potential topics in mind. Previewing will let you know if you've defined a topic too broadly or too narrowly. It will also give you a sense of whether or not you have access to the resources the topic would require. If your library does not have some of the key journals or books, you'll need to use interlibrary loan (which can take six weeks or more; see Chapter 8) or redefine your subject.

As you preview the literature, you will be building a working bibliography as well as skimming abstracts and perhaps articles to determine their value for your paper. Don't take the time to read the full article at this point (you'll get to that step once you've committed yourself to a topic). But do record each reference in full APA format (see Chapter 9) on a separate 3″ × 5″ card or piece of paper so that you'll be able to retrieve that information and sort and alphabetize the references you actually use when you ultimately construct your reference list.

Previewing the literature will not only tell you about the quantity of information available, but will also give you a sense of its *quality*. As you preview the literature, take note of the types of references on hand:

1. Are they **primary** sources (that is, authored by the originator of the ideas or data) or are they **secondary** sources (exclusively reporting the work of others)? You should obtain primary sources whenever possible, since they allow you to interpret the information as it was originally presented. On the other hand, if you find the primary sources confusing, secondary sources may help clarify the material, but be certain to cite that secondary source (see Chapter 9). In particular, published literature reviews (in journals or books) can be an excellent source; they are secondary sources in that they review the material of others, but are primary sources in terms of their original synthesis of that material. Literature reviews can be found in many professional journals and edited books. *Psychological Bulletin,* a journal published by the American Psychological Association, and the *Annual Review of Psychology,* a yearly edited volume, include literature reviews on a broad range of topics in psychology.

2. Are the sources professional journal articles, books, or magazine articles from the popular media? Unless your instructor feels otherwise, it's often best to focus upon professional journal articles. These primary sources generally are written in a more concise and clear format, and have passed the stringent review of other professionals before being published. Edited books may also contain primary source chapters which succinctly summarize relevant research, although the research may not be scrutinized as carefully as in some journals. Non-edited books may contain important information, and may involve primary or secondary source material. However, their length and structure often make it more difficult to extract information. Popular magazine articles may be primary or secondary sources (commonly they are the latter). Their major disadvantage is that, because they are typically directed to the lay reader, they often omit many details or simplify complex findings that are crucial to your analysis of a writer's position.

3. Is the information **empirical** or **theoretical?** The initial excitement students feel after compiling a long list of references can turn to frustration with the discovery that the references are all theoretical rather than empirical. There is nothing wrong with doing a paper on theoretical material. However, if your assignment is to review **empirical research** in an area, you must be sensitive to the distinction between theoretical and empirical work. Empirical information is that which is based on experiment or observation — ideas which have been tested. There are many topics that have fostered interesting speculation and even theory, but not all of them have been examined systematically in an empirical manner.

WRITING 5.3: PREVIEWING THE LITERATURE. For two of the topics you defined in Writing 5.2, find ten to fifteen references (using the library research techniques explained in Chapter 8). Once you've considered the quantity and quality of the resources available, select one of these as the topic for your literature review (or, if necessary, preview the literature for another topic from your cluster diagram). In your journal, or on a separate piece of paper, make a list of what you know about your topic already. Make another list of the questions you'd like to answer about your topic.

Defining the Purpose of Your Paper

An important part of defining your topic is deciding upon the **purpose** of your paper. Here are some of the most common types of literature reviews:

1. **State-of-the-art review.** This is the form that student papers

most commonly take. This review responds to the question, "What is our current understanding of this topic?"

2. **Historical review.** This approach traces the evolution of the way in which a topic has been conceptualized and/or researched over a period of time.

3. **Comparison of perspectives.** The writer focuses on a few select perspectives on an issue, and relies on comparison and contrast procedures to clarify similarities and dissimilarities, and perhaps to synthesize different viewpoints.

4. **Reinterpretation of x in terms of y.** This type of paper may require a sophisticated understanding of the topic as well as related topics. The writer reinterprets the findings in one area (x) in light of information gleaned from another area (y). An example would be to reinterpret the literature on problem-solving skills among the elderly in light of research on risk-taking behavior of the elderly. It may be that the elderly's problem-solving abilities don't decline with age, but rather the elderly may become slower to respond simply because they become less willing to risk making a mistake.

5. **Theory or model building.** The writer attempts to construct a theory or model which pulls together the literature topic. This is a complex and sophisticated task which generally requires considerable breadth and depth of knowledge in the field.

Don't feel bound by this list — it's neither rigid nor comprehensive. Literature reviews are sometimes based on a combination of these approaches or are designed with an alternative goal. Carefully consider the requirements of your specific assignment and within those constraints be as imaginative as you like. But remember that even the most creative paper requires a clearly defined purpose.

It should be obvious that some types of literature reviews require knowledge and analytical skills which students are not expected to have early in their training. However, others (state-of-the-art, historical, comparison) are feasible approaches for a student new to a field. In any case, your choice of paper topic and purpose will be intimately linked. For example, certain topics have a rich historical past; others do not. Some topics involve clearly defined, conflicting perspectives; others do not. Previewing the literature will help you to determine what type of literature review is most feasible, given your topic. At the same time, as you define the purpose of your paper, you may need to reshape your topic.

In fact, defining topic and purpose is not a one-step decision but rather is an ongoing **process.** Although it is important to focus upon a particular topic and purpose once you have previewed the literature, you will undoubtedly continue to modify each as you proceed with reviewing and analyzing the literature.

WRITING 5.4: DEFINING THE PURPOSE OF YOUR PAPER. Based upon your preview of the literature, list the types of review approaches that seem feasible for your topic. Considering how appropriate and how interesting each approach appears to you, select the one you tentatively will use for your paper.

Reviewing the Literature

You've already assembled a working bibliography to allow you to preview the literature. Now you should return to those references and read, read, read. Frankly, the best approach is to begin by spending several days reading through your sources without taking any formal notes. Just try to get a broadly based understanding of the topic. While this approach requires some time "up front," we're convinced that it saves you much more time in the long run. Without acquiring this general background on your topic, you'll spend a great deal of time taking tedious notes that will prove unnecessary for your paper.

On the other hand, this preliminary review of the literature is a perfect opportunity to take advantage of your journal (see Chapter 2). Use it to note questions and general impressions, to synthesize the material, to determine what you do and don't understand, and to speculate on possible directions for your work. By the time you are ready to draft your paper, these journal entries may well help you to organize the material you've been reading as well as to find the language to describe it.

Next, carefully and systematically read through your sources one by one, analyzing what each can contribute to your paper. In attempting to draw information from each source, keep in mind the **purpose** or **goal** of your literature review. Also consider your **audience;** unless told otherwise, write for an individual who is familiar with common psychological terms, but not an expert on your subject. Both the purpose and the audience of your paper will influence which aspects of sources will be most relevant to you. As you read carefully, you may also find yourself reformulating your topic and/or purpose a bit. That's fine. The structure of your paper should certainly be responsive to what is available in the literature. As you read you should also keep adding references to your working bibliography (continuing to record each in APA format on a separate 3″ × 5″ piece of paper). Regardless of how systematically you have searched for resources in the library, you'll undoubtedly come upon a few new citations in your reading. If you find yourself continuing to discover a large number of new references, it's likely that your library search was not sufficiently thorough. Reread Chapter 8 and try again!

Taking *good* notes is a challenging and underrated skill. If this statement surprises you, then it's likely that you are not doing all the thinking you should when taking notes. Simply transcribing information from library resources to your own paper is not enough. Taking good notes requires that you first *integrate* the new information into your framework of understanding. Therefore, it's best to read the entire article before beginning to take notes (and even better to respond first to the article in your journal). After you've digested the material, put it into your *own* words on note cards. Do not quote or paraphrase the original source unless there is a compelling reason to do so (for example, if the author articulated a certain point in a particularly powerful way). Papers which consist of a series of quotations can suggest that the writer was unable to develop or integrate the material on his or her own. If you do include quotations or paraphrasing in your notes, be certain to record the page number(s) from which they were taken; you'll need to cite those pages in your text. Chapter 4 discusses procedures for writing summaries, Chapter 8 offers explicit advice on taking notes, and Chapter 9 provides the format for APA citations.

While photocopying machines have made it relatively inexpensive to make personal copies of all the resources for your paper, beware! There are real dangers in this, many of which you've probably already experienced. When you have a photocopy of an article, it's easier to postpone reading it — somehow having the pile of photocopies in hand makes you feel like you've done the work. You're also less likely to take thoughtful notes since you've always got the article to turn to. And when the time comes to draft your paper, it's more difficult to translate the information into your own words when you've got the author's words staring at you. So, our advice to you is to save your money and write a better paper.

WRITING 5.5: TAKING NOTES. Review Chapter 8's guidelines for taking notes. Then, after taking notes on three different sources, exchange your note cards with a classmate. Compare the structure and level of detail you each incorporated; discuss the advantages and disadvantages of each style. Even if you've used different references, a comparison of note-taking styles can teach you a great deal.

Analyzing the Literature Toward Drafting Your Review

Now that you've developed a clearer vision of your paper, you need to commit yourself to an **audience, voice,** and **purpose** (introduced in Chapter 1). For whom will you write, who will you be as you write, and what approach (or purpose) have you selected? Note how these questions and their answers typically evolve in an interrelated and gradual fashion.

With the purpose or approach of your paper decided, you should organize your notes to correspond with the approach. If you have decided to take a time-oriented or historical approach, you'll need to rearrange your note cards in a chronological sequence. If you are taking a state-of-the-art approach, you should order your note cards to reflect the issues they address in a hierarchical fashion, much like an outline. Divide them first according to main issues, and then subdivide each of those sets of notes by subissues, and so on. Now, you should construct an outline or table of contents. Creating your outline and reshuffling your note cards will actually be interdependent processes. Your outline will shape the way in which you organize your notes, but sorting through your notes will undoubtedly lead to modifications in your outline.

Your paper should be organized *conceptually* rather than by your sources of information; that is, it should be organized according to central issues or ideas. When using a time-oriented or historical approach, portray the historical changes in terms of their evolving conceptual emphases. One of the most common mistakes of student writers is to organize papers by source, simply reporting one source after another; for example:

```
Jones (1982) found that. . . . An interesting study
by Smith & Kamarsky (1965) reported. . . . Then
Sooza (1986) argued. . . . Another study (Beatrix,
1977) revealed. . . .
```

This type of pattern leads the reader to ask, "So what? Where are you going?" and "What's your point?" In fact, in a good literature review, any one reference might be cited at several very different points in the text, whenever it is relevant to the *issue* being addressed. Impose *your* organization upon the material rather than passively follow the organization of each of your sources in succession.

Your paper should also reflect an **integration** and **synthesis** of the material. Regardless of the purpose you define for your paper, you are responsible for formulating a question or issue and pursuing it actively and directly. Even in a time-oriented or historical review, you should be contributing more than a summary of each source in historical sequence — in this case, you should be making some point about the evolution of thinking in the field.

> WRITING 5.6: ORGANIZING YOUR PAPER. Construct a rough outline for your review, keeping the topic, purpose, and audience of your paper in mind. Use this outline to draft an informal, two-page summary of what your paper will cover (make it a letter to a friend). This will help you to discover the strengths and weaknesses of your outline, and language for discussing your ideas.

In analyzing literature, consider the relative merits of the arguments or positions you've read. As Chapter 3 explains (in the section on argument/evaluation), consider both the **quantity** and

quality of evidence. A few examples of supporting evidence from highly credible sources can be far more convincing than a mass of evidence from questionable sources. Examine the degree to which there is consensus among different researchers on a particular point — consensus adds credibility. Consider whether varied research methodologies arrive at the same conclusions (or if the consistency or inconsistency in results can be explained by the similarities and dissimilarities in approaches). Pay attention to the theoretical assumptions made by authors and the ways in which variables are operationally defined.

Carefully examine the controversies in the literature — they make papers much more exciting. And you may find you are able to explain conflicting findings by attending to the different assumptions, definitions, subjects, or procedures used.

As you proceed through your analysis of the literature, jot down your thoughts on separate cards (see Chapter 8) so that you can sort and organize them with your other note cards. It's amazing how many brilliant flashes get lost if you don't record them immediately, and these notes on your thoughts will be equally, if not more, important than your research notes. Be certain to go carefully through your personal journal as well, transferring relevant ideas to note cards which can be integrated with your source material.

Chapter 3's section on argument and evaluation addresses many of the issues involved in evaluating evidence. Take a look at it.

WRITING 5.7: ANALYZING THE LITERATURE: EVALUATING YOUR INFORMATION. Organize your note cards into separate piles to correspond with your outline. For each major section (that is, for each group of cards), list the varieties of sources, research methodologies, and populations studied. Consider the significance of the variability you've discovered.

DRAFTING YOUR PAPER: PAPER FORMAT

Most literature reviews have three main parts: the title, the body of the text, and the reference list. Some also include an abstract preceding the body of the paper.

Title Page

Your title page may vary depending upon whether you are submitting your paper for publication or for a course. According to the APA (1983) publication format, you should begin your paper with a separate title page that includes the paper's title, your name and institutional affiliation (e.g., your school), and a running head (an abbreviated title, of no more than fifty characters, which would be typed on the top of each page of the article if it were published). At the top right corner of this (and every) page, type the first two or three words of your title. This "short title" allows the reader to identify the pages of your manuscript if they become separated. If you are submitting your paper for an assignment, your instructor may not require a running head but may, instead, want you to add the date and the purpose for which the paper was submitted (e.g., your course title or an Honor's thesis). Figure 5.2 is an example of a title page in APA format and Figure 5.3 is an alternative form for a student paper (see pages 86 and 87).

Your title should be a concise summary of the main idea of the paper and the issues or variables examined. Include only those words which contribute to achieving this goal. An example of a poor title is

> An Examination of the Effects of Different Types of Stereotyping on College Students' Course Grades in School

An improved title would be

> The Impact of Stereotyping on College Academic Success

Abstract

The construction of an abstract is described in detail in Chapter 4. The abstract for a literature review assigned for a course can be brief, but it should follow the same guidelines for structure and content as those designed for publications. Since your abstract is a concise but comprehensive summary of your entire literature review, it's best to write it after you've completed your paper.

Body

The body of your paper actually is composed of three sections: the introduction, the main text, and your summary or conclusions.

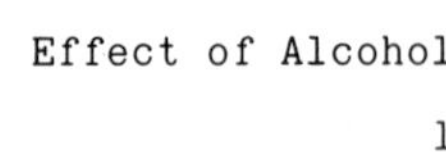

The Effect of Alcohol Content on Taste Preference
in Humans

Gary L. Bond

Carion College

Running head: EFFECT OF ALCOHOL CONTENT ON TASTE
PREFERENCE

Figure 5.2 *Title page in APA format* (Running head: Effect of Alcohol Content on Taste Preference)

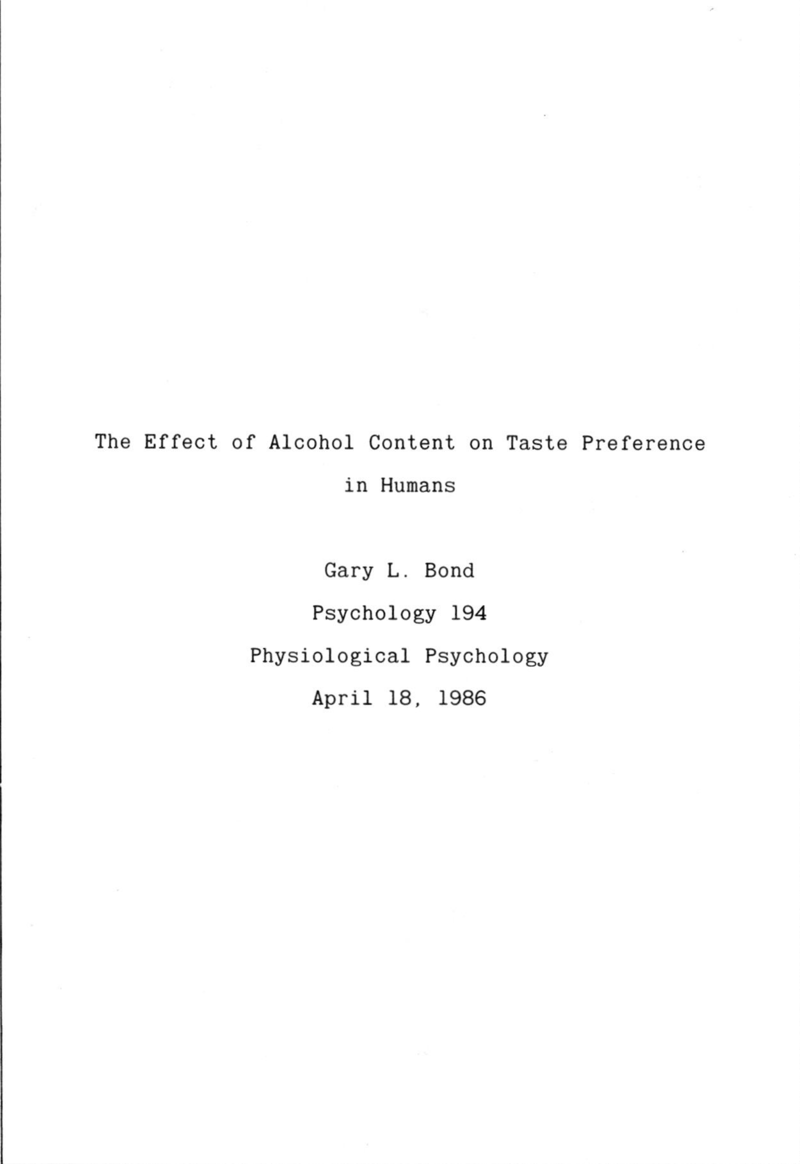

The Effect of Alcohol Content on Taste Preference in Humans

Gary L. Bond

Psychology 194

Physiological Psychology

April 18, 1986

Figure 5.3 *Alternative title page format*

However, these are usually informal sections and typically are *not* labeled. On the other hand, the use of these and any other headings (and subheadings) is at the discretion of the author; they may provide greater clarity.

The introduction of a ten- to fifteen-page literature review may be just one or two paragraphs in length. Its purpose is to orient the reader to the topic and present a clear statement of the problem or issue to be addressed. The introduction should also specify the approach the paper will take (historical, state-of-the-art, comparison of opposing views, etc.). The introduction can often be used to provide your reader with an overview of your entire thesis; however, skilled writers sometimes will begin by stating opposing arguments and only gradually present their thesis as the paper unfolds.

Here is the introduction from a student paper on "The Effects of Father Absence on Children's Cognitive Development."

The Effects of Father Absence on Children's Cognitive Development

The issue of father absence is one of growing concern in modern American society because of its increasing prevalence. In the span of years between 1970 and 1978, for example, the number of children living in father-absent homes increased from 10 to 15 percent (U.S. Census Bureau, 1978). The relationship between father-absence and cognitive development is particularly important because of its implications for the success and well-being of people in an increasingly complicated world. The purpose of this paper is to provide a comprehensive and critical review of our current understanding of the relationship between father-absence and child cognitive growth.

The main text is the meat of your paper — a presentation of the substance of your review. This is where you integrate and analyze the research in a coherent, logical progression. Drafting the body of your paper should not be particularly difficult if you've done a thorough job in the prewriting phase. However, one of the most important tasks in composing a literature review is maintaining a focused thesis. Your introduction should have clearly defined the thesis for your reader. While your review will likely examine various facets of your central theme, be cautious not to overextend your analysis. You can't say everything, so describe only that information which is directly relevant to your theme. If you try to include too much, your paper will appear disorganized and superficial. If you keep your scope limited and your thesis in front of you, your draft will be easier to write and more coherent.

Here are some sample pages of the main text of the student paper on "Effects of Father Absence on Children's Cognitive Development":

> A number of studies have suggested a relationship between father-absence and deficits in scholastic achievement, particularly among boys (e.g., Deutsch, 1960). For example, it was found that urban school children from father-absent families performed more poorly than children from father-present homes, even when the subject groups were matched for socioeconomic status (Deutsch & Brown, 1964). That this finding is not simply a result of child trauma concerning father death or divorce is suggested by the work of Blanchard and Biller (1971). They found that boys whose fathers interacted with them an average of more than two hours per day performed superior to father-absent boys <u>and</u> boys whose fathers were available fewer than six hours per week. Since Blanchard and Biller matched their subjects for I.Q. scores, their findings refute Kohlberg's (1966) contention that the differences in the group are due to differences in intelligence. Instead, they argued that the father-present boys were "more likely to actualize their intellectual potential" (p. 304) which supports Deutsch's (1960) view that motivation to achieve is higher in father-present children.
>
> However, both type and timing of father-absence have been found to influence its effects on children's scholastic achievement (e.g., Hetherington, 1966; Radin, 1981; Santrock, 1970, 1972). Children who lost their fathers through non-death-related events (divorce, separation, or desertion) before the age of five were more harmed than six to eleven year olds who lost their fathers for the same reasons (Radin, 1981; Santrock, 1972). The

loss had a particularly damaging effect if it occurred before the child was two. However, when father-absence was due to death, boys were most vulnerable between the ages of six and nine. In fact, death of the father in the first two years of life was associated with a trend toward a higher I.Q. (Santrock, 1972). In the case of paternal death, according to Santrock (1972), mothers may consciously encourage their children to become someone of whom their deceased husbands would have been proud.

The effects of a stepfather entering the household also vary, depending upon the child's age. . . .

The conclusion of a ten- to fifteen-page literature review usually requires no more than a paragraph, assuming that you've been integrating the information through the paper. Use the summary to do more than simply restate what you've already said; try to present a clear and concise synthesis of your analysis. Here is the conclusion from the student paper on "Effects of Father Absence on Children's Cognitive Development":

In conclusion, while there is some agreement regarding the effects of father-absence on cognitive development, the relationships between these factors seem complex and indirect. Effects vary depending upon the way in which cognitive development is assessed, and even within any one mode of assessment, effects vary with the cause of the father-absence, its timing, and the sex of the child. Furthermore, it may not be simply father-absence itself which affects the child. Rather, it may be that certain types of father-absence lead to other factors which can influence the child's cognitive development, such as financial stress, mother's emotional stress, and even poor nutrition. It now seems most important to develop research which analyzes the mediators of the effects of father-absence (such as a mother's reactions to the father's absence). This understanding should help resolve contradictions within the existing literature as well as help us to develop interventions which could prevent some of the detrimental effects.

References

Your reference list should start on a new page, following the body of your paper, and be numbered consecutively with the main text. Assembling this list should be quite simple if you've been recording each reference in APA format on a 3″ × 5″ reference card (as suggested in Chapter 8). All you'll need to do is to go carefully through the citations in your paper and select the corresponding reference cards. Be sure that every reference cited in your paper is included in your reference list. Don't include sources which you read but didn't cite unless your instructor specifically requests you to do so. It's best to construct your reference list *after* you've completed (but not typed) the final draft of your paper, since citations get added and deleted during the revision process. Be certain that authors and dates in your citations are consistent with those on your cards. Refer to Chapter 9 for details on structuring the reference list.

Appendixes

It is rare that you will include appendixes, but you may find them helpful or even required for some assignments. Appendixes should only be used for supplementary information, that is, information which may be useful but is not essential for the understanding of the paper. Examples include a copy of a questionnaire or detailed subject instructions. Appendixes are labeled by capital letters (A, B, C, etc.) in the order in which they are mentioned in the text. You can refer to appendixes in your text in the following way:

```
. . . difficult questions (see Appendix A for the
complete questionnaire)
```

Tables and Figures

Certain information is more effectively presented in a table or figure (e.g., a graph) than in the text. For example, some literature reviews will include a table that compares groups of studies on the basis of their procedures and/or results. Other reviews will present a figure of an experimental apparatus commonly used in the literature rather than attempt to describe it in words. Tables and figures are numbered separately from one another (e.g., a paper can have both a Table 1 and a Figure 1) and consecutively in the order in which they are introduced in the text. If your instructor asks you to use APA publication format (APA, 1983), do not place tables and figures directly in the text. Rather, type each on a separate page and place them in numerical order (first all the tables, then all the figures) following the reference list and any appendixes. Refer to a table or figure in your text by its number:

```
. . . was related to drug strength (see Table 3)

. . . as outlined in Table 2, there are important
differences . . .

Figure 1 illustrates . . .
```

When using APA format, indicate approximately where the table or figure belongs in the text by inserting the following between the appropriate lines:

```
-------------------------
Insert Table 3 about here
-------------------------
```

Information on preparing tables and figures is detailed in Chapter 7. Be certain to read that section before including either in your literature review.

If you use a table or figure from another source, you must cite the original author(s). Do so by citing the reference in a general note at the bottom of the table or at the end of the figure caption (see Chapter 7):

From The nation's families: 1960–1990 by G. Masnick & M. J. Bane, 1980.

WRITING 5.8: DRAFTING YOUR LITERATURE REVIEW. Using the outline you created in Writing 5.6, write a full draft of your paper. Be certain that you have met the requirements of each individual section of the paper (title, abstract, body, references, appendixes, tables, figures), but don't worry about details like spelling, punctuation, and word choice at this point.

REVISING YOUR PAPER

You may think of revision as something you do if you find yourself with spare time after you've "finished" your paper. Revision is actually an essential part of the writing process, and unless you schedule time for revision, you'll find yourself unable to *finish* your paper in the true sense. Revision is essential not only for polishing your sentence structure and spelling, but also for polishing your *thinking!* Rereading a full draft allows you to evaluate connections, logic, and organization which you couldn't see before.

So, does revision simply mean rereading your paper? Well, to *revise* does literally mean to *see again*. But there are a few simple steps you can take to make the revision process more productive:

1. Get away from your paper for a while. When you've just finished composing a paper, much of it is still in your head, making it difficult to think about it from a fresh perspective. If you wait a couple of days, then you'll be better able to approach it as a new reader — and that's who you want to be sure will understand it! Even if you don't have a few days to spare, an hour or two of distraction will help. Go eat dinner, or take a run, or watch some mindless television — do anything that will get your mind somewhere else.

2. Begin with more global revisions and gradually work to the finer details. Don't focus on sentence structure and choice of words your first time through. Instead, begin by reading your paper *from start to finish* and considering whether it has a clear logic and organization. Why spend ten minutes debating about the use of this or that word when the whole paragraph may not fit with the flow of the paper? Once you feel comfortable that your paper presents a clear statement and a coherent organization, then begin working on revising subsections, paragraphs, and finally sentences.

3. Have a friend read your paper. When you've put so much time and thought into researching an area, it's quite easy to make assumptions which a naive reader may not make or understand. What appears clear and logical to you may be confusing and unreasonable to even a well-versed reader who has come to understand the topic from different perspectives than yours. That's why most professional writers ask a colleague to read their work before they are willing to call it finished. Feedback from a friend will help you anticipate the feedback you might get from an instructor or editor.

4. Once your paper is typed, proofread it! It is very distracting to read a poorly typed paper. Even if you have your paper professionally typed, be certain to proofread it. Ask a friend to proofread it as well. You are likely to read the paper as you wrote it rather than as it was typed. A sloppy paper with typographical errors can give the impression of sloppy thinking. It's difficult to have much confidence in a paper that does not seem to have been completed with care.

5. Photocopy your paper. Instructors are human, and so are you. Papers can get misplaced. Therefore, always photocopy your papers.

WRITING 5.9: REVISING YOUR PAPER. Get away from your paper for at least a few hours, preferably for a few days. Then revise, following our guidelines. Have a friend read your paper (you could exchange papers with a classmate) and use the feedback to complete your final draft.

CHECKLIST FOR WRITING A LITERATURE REVIEW

Prewriting

1. Is your *topic* narrow enough to be covered comprehensively, but broad enough to allow an integrative review of material?
2. Have you *systematically searched* for sources relevant to your topic?
3. Have you *carefully read and taken notes* from all your sources before beginning to write a draft?
4. Have you defined the *purpose* of your review, that is, the *approach* you are going to take?
5. Have you *analyzed and organized* your information into a coherent and integrated structure which is appropriate to the goal of the paper?

Drafting

6. Is your *title* a concise but accurate summary of the central issues in your paper?
7. Does your *abstract* accurately summarize the scope and conclusions of your paper?
8. Does the *body* of your paper
   a. include a clear statement of the purpose and goal of the paper?
   b. follow a consistent organization throughout?
   c. include all the important sources on the topic?
   d. integrate, rather than simply report, information from your sources?
   e. cite your sources according to APA guidelines?
   f. refer to tables, figures, and appendixes in an appropriate manner?
   g. include a conclusion which logically emerges from the content and organization of the paper?
9. Does your *reference list*
   a. include every source which was cited in the body of the paper and no others?
   b. list references in alphabetical order?
   c. cite each source in its proper format?
10. Are *appendixes, tables* and *figures* properly identified and sequenced as cited in the body of your paper?

Revising

11. Have you gotten some distance from your paper before returning to revise?
12. Have you worked from more global to finer levels of revision?
13. Have you had a friend read your final draft?

Once it has been typed, *have you proofread your paper?*
Have you photocopied your paper?

[6] *The Research Proposal*

PREVIEW:

"How can you possibly study with the radio going?" If you haven't been asked this question yourself, you've probably asked it of someone else. When it comes time to concentrate on something, most people turn the music off, but some turn it on. What does music do to the ability to concentrate? Does it depend on whether the music is rock, country, or classical? Does it depend on the listener?

The **scientific method** begins with precisely this sort of observation and questioning. The scientist then tries to answer the questions. The scientific method involves:

1. Making an observation: Some people listen to music when they study, others do not.

2. **Raising questions** regarding the observation: What are the effects of different types of music on different people?

3. **Formulating an hypothesis** or explanation: Perhaps the degree to which music distracts or focuses attention depends upon one's mood and familiarity with the music.

4. **Testing the hypothesis by experimentation:** For example, expose people in different moods to music which varies in familiarity, and measure ability to concentrate.

5. **Formulating a scientific theory** if your hypothesis is repeatedly confirmed in this and other experiments.

In reality, experiments usually present more questions than answers and lead the researcher to revise the original hypotheses and redesign the experiment. The continual refining of questions and methodological design is an important product of the experimental process.

THE RESEARCH PROPOSAL: WHAT IS IT AND WHY WRITE IT?

As its name suggests, the research proposal **proposes** a new experiment and consists of three major sections: (a) an **introduction** — the rationale for the study and relevant observations, questions, and hypotheses; (b) a **method** — the procedure for conducting and analyzing the experiment; and usually (c) **results/discussion** — a description of the expected results and their interpretation. Professionals usually develop a research proposal in preparation for conducting an actual experiment. However, writing a proposal can be a powerful learning experience even if you never plan to do the research. You are forced to go beyond what is known to think about what is possible using hypothetical, deductive, and causal reasoning. Moreover, writing a proposal helps you to develop *techniques* for problem-finding, problem-solving, and communication. Without these activities, science would stagnate; knowledge would reach a standstill.

Consider three general functions served by writing a research proposal:

1. Research proposals **allow you to communicate your ideas to others** so that they can learn from you and can evaluate and/or provide feedback regarding your thinking. When researchers ask foundations or government agencies for financial support, they submit research proposals in order to be evaluated and get suggestions for modifications. Students are asked to write research proposals for the same reasons, even in situations when they are not required to do the actual experiment.

2. Writing a proposal **is a process that can develop and refine your thinking.** Even when you feel you've got a clear idea of a research project in your head, the process of writing it down reveals gaps and inconsistencies in your logic. It also helps you attend to the details which ultimately determine whether the experiment has any value. Professional researchers as well as students discover this each time they write a proposal.

3. Constructing a research proposal **promotes general problem-solving skills** which should serve you far beyond the writing of this particular proposal. The proposal requires you to achieve breadth and depth of understanding, and to create a synthesis of previous literature in the field. You exercise skills of logic and analysis as you construct hypotheses, articulate an experimental design, and anticipate an interpretation of results. These skills are not only basic to education but will extend beyond this particular paper, this course, and your role as a student.

The remainder of this chapter will discuss the procedures for developing a research proposal. They involve defining your experimental question (including selecting a topic, previewing the literature, and defining the scope of your question), reviewing and analyzing the literature, drafting the proposal, and revising. The preliminary (prewriting) steps resemble those discussed in Chapter 5, The Literature Review. Review relevant sections from that chapter. Although we'll summarize some of the procedures that are common to other assignments as well, we'll emphasize the ways in which the research proposal is unique. We won't try to describe all the issues involved in experimental *design*. You'll find, however, that effective writing strategies also lead to better research plans.

DEFINING YOUR EXPERIMENTAL QUESTION

The process of defining your research question is just that — a *process*. Keep an open mind. Your question should continue to evolve as you read, talk with others, write in your journal, and daydream. On one hand, it's important to restrict your focus — you can't make progress until you're willing to set a course. On the other hand, don't become too attached to a specific question and/or method right away. You'll see that it's important to allow your ideas to build upon the thoughts and experiences of others.

What do you do if you don't know where to begin? Your instructor has given you some guidelines, but your choices remain wide open. The first thing you need to do is narrow your choices down to a specific subject. Don't worry about defining your actual *question* for now — just begin by selecting a topic.

Selecting a Topic

Selecting a topic for research is much like selecting a topic for any assignment. If your instructor provides you with a list of topics from which to choose, you can base your choice on personal interest. If your choices are not so restricted, you can follow those steps we discussed in Chapter 5:

1. **Turn to your journal.** If you've been making regular entries in your journal, it can be a valuable source of research topics. Pay particular attention to entries in which you've raised questions, expressed disagreement, or noticed controversies and contradictions.

2. **Browse through your textbooks.** In particular, notice which areas seem controversial or incomplete. An introductory psychology text can be particularly helpful if your assignment isn't restricted to a specific area (in a course on general experimental methods, for example).

3. **Skim abstracts and professional journals.** Focus on the most current journals to get a sense of the "hot" issues. You might also

take note of topics in which authors are rebutting the work of others.

4. Scan through your lecture notes. Instructors usually try to mention current controversies in the field. If your topic is not restricted to a particular area of psychology, look through your notes from previous courses.

Whatever area you choose, be certain that it's of interest to you! One of the best indicators of a good topic is that it deals with what you think are important and intriguing questions. If you're not excited about the subject, you'll have a more difficult time exciting your reader.

WRITING 6.1: FINDING A TOPIC. Using the techniques described above (and in Chapter 5), find three possible research topics that meet your course requirements. Then turn to your journal (or a piece of paper), and for each topic, spend five minutes brainstorming relevant questions, writing what you know and don't know. Which topic raises the most interesting issues for you? Don't commit yourself to a specific question now — this is just preliminary thinking.

Previewing the Literature

Once you have a general topic, use the techniques described in Chapter 8 (Principles of Library Research) to identify relevant sources. Preview the literature available in the subject area to define a specific research question. Don't try to analyze the details of the literature at this time. For now your goals are to (a) establish whether there is any research and theory relevant to the topic; (b) discover the general kinds of questions that have been asked in the area; (c) become familiar with prominent theories and findings on your topic; and (d) identify current controversies and questions in the area.

Certain types of reading can be more beneficial than others for identifying a research question. As Sternberg (1977) suggests:

1. Start with more general references and work toward specific readings; you need to begin by establishing a firm base of knowledge from which to work.

2. Read in depth on a few selected topics rather than superficially on several; only in-depth analyses will provide the sorts of insights necessary to identify a meaningful question.

3. Read the most current literature in the area; otherwise, you may find yourself "reinventing the wheel" — examining a question which has long been answered or has been discarded because it did not prove useful.

Published literature reviews are a tremendous resource for identifying research questions. These reviews can be found in many research journals and edited books. *Psychological Bulletin,* a journal published by the American Psychological Association, and the *Annual Review of Psychology,* a yearly edited volume, include literature reviews on a broad range of psychology topics. As mentioned in Chapter 5, literature reviews can identify general trends that aren't necessarily reflected in individual studies. They can offer alternative interpretations of research findings, resolve controversies by comparing groups of investigations by research design or treatment format, highlight inconsistencies in the methodologies and findings of previous research, and teach general lessons about research design factors that influence outcomes. For these reasons, many instructors assign students the task of writing an in-depth literature review paper preliminary to the research proposal.

As you read through the literature, experiment with different strategies for developing your research question. Sternberg (1977, pp. 41–43) illustrated several of these:

> Suppose, for example, that you read an article testing the theory that repeated exposure to persuasive communications results in attitude change toward the viewpoint advocated by those communications, regardless of one's initial attitudes. You might pursue further research taking you in any one of four directions:
>
> (1) *Extend the theory.* After reading the article, you may be persuaded that the theory is sound and could be extended. You might want to show that repeated exposure to communications advocating a viewpoint, but in a nonpersuasive manner, also results in attitude change toward the position taken by the communications.
>
> (2) *Generate an analogous theory.* If you find the theory and

data compelling, you may want to think up an analogous theory. Perhaps repeated exposure to a particular kind of music increases liking for that music. Or perhaps repeated exposure to any kind of communication increases positive affect toward that kind of communication.

(3) *Limit the theory.* Perhaps you believe that the conclusion derived from the data is too broad. If the subjects in the experiment were all children, for example, you may wish to show that the theory is applicable only to children. Or if the communications used in the experiment were all health-related ones, you may want to show that the theory is applicable only to arguments related to bodily care.

(4) *Challenge the evidence testing the theory.* In reading the article, you may spot a methodological, statistical, or logical flaw in the author's argument. In this case, you may want to test the theory in a way that corrects the flaw. For example, suppose that the author of the paper tested his or her hypothesis merely by showing that after two hours of listening to a set of three persuasive communications, most subjects agreed with the viewpoint advocated by those communications. If the author has not shown, however, that at least some of his or her subjects disagreed with the viewpoints of the communications prior to the test, then the conclusion does not follow from his or her data.

Of course, you needn't rely solely on your reading for ideas. Draw on these as well:

Personal experiences and observations — e.g., noticing that one of your neighbors turns his stereo on when he studies, while another turns his off.

Folk-wisdom — e.g., questioning familiar proverbs: "familiarity breeds contempt," or does it?

Problems you encounter day-to-day — e.g., can we train ourselves not to procrastinate?

Informal writing you find around you — like this series of bathroom graffitti from a women's dormitory:

You can't have love where there isn't friendship.
Yes you can!!!!
You're thinking of lust.

> How can you possibly love someone you don't consider your friend?
> Love and hate are the same emotion.
> You can make your lover your friend but don't make a friend your lover.

This interchange, which a student had recorded on a MacDonald's bag and inserted in her journal, led to a research proposal on the relationship between sexual attraction and friendship.

In defining the scope of your question, don't bite off more than you can chew! One of the most common mistakes of new researchers is to try to ask too much. After reviewing the literature you realize that there is actually an entire set of related questions that need to be asked. It's tempting — and a mistake — to try to answer them all in a single study. Scientific knowledge grows by integrating the findings of successive research; any single experiment can't adequately address all the questions. Therefore, limit yourself to one or two important issues. For example, introduce a *single* new variable to a relationship you wish to explore. Limit the ages of your subjects, their species, their gender, the behavioral context of interest (e.g., academic performance). While the other related questions may be important ones to raise, it's unlikely that your study will be practical, manageable, or interpretable if you try to deal with them all.

"Can I replicate someone else's study with minor modifications?" This is probably the most common question students ask about research proposals. As you'll see, research *should* build on earlier studies, directly when possible, and indirectly when not. Moreover, the work of a top researcher may well consist of a series of studies which are basically replications with minor, but systematic, modifications of previous work. But use your head. If the proposal is a course assignment and intended to promote and assess your analytical skills, creativity, and understanding of the field, a direct replication with minor modifications is not likely to be particularly impressive — unless that "minor" modification actually reflects a major, insightful contribution.

WRITING 6.2: DEFINING YOUR EXPERIMENTAL QUESTION. Based on your daily observations, your preview of the literature, and your journal entries, develop three different research questions that relate to your topic. For each of these questions, spend ten minutes writing in your journal about ways in which you might experimentally pose the question and the results you would expect to find. Then decide which experimental question you find most interesting and promising.

REVIEWING AND ANALYZING THE LITERATURE

Those who are new to research often underestimate the importance of using literature to develop a proposal, particularly when they arrive at their research question without mulling through published sources. But once you've identified a question, you need to review relevant theory and research carefully and systematically. The process involved is much like that detailed in Chapter 5. To summarize:

1. Identify relevant references using the techniques described in Chapter 8. Start with the most recent abstracts and citation indexes and work backwards in time. Record each reference in full APA format (see Chapter 9) on a separate 3″ × 5″ card.

2. Preview the references without taking notes; just try to get a sense of the questions, methods, results, and conclusions of others. Pay attention to the references cited in your sources and add them to your working bibliography, if appropriate. If you reviewed the literature in order to define your research question, you may have completed much of this literature preview already. Nevertheless, check your note cards and sources to be sure that your search has been thorough.

3. Carefully read each of your sources. Analyze what each can contribute to your proposal, and take notes on this information (Chapter 8 includes suggestions for note-taking). Incorporate the information into your own framework of understanding before you write it down, then record it in your own words. This makes your job much easier when the time comes to draft your proposal.

As you read and analyze the literature, you'll likely revise your research question. That's fine. Your experimental question should be responsive to, and grow from, the current body of knowledge.

Do you need to go to the literature if you already think you know precisely what you want to ask and how you want to ask it? Yes. Although you can develop a research proposal without reviewing the literature, you can't develop a *good* one. The goal of research is to advance the current state of knowledge. Given the limited scope of any single experiment, a study contributes most when it has a clear and logical relationship to previous research. This connection allows the study to produce more than isolated findings; it expands our understanding of an entire body of related research. Therefore, never become too attached to a single issue and/or method until after you've carefully and thoroughly read and analyzed the literature. Once you've completed this analysis, then ask yourself, "What's the next question that needs to be raised and, based on past experience, how should it be asked?"

If your proposed study is going to contribute to the current state of knowledge, your analysis of existing literature should involve asking different types of questions:

1. To what extent has your question and/or related questions been considered by other researchers? Can your question be modified to complement this history?

2. How have others developed hypotheses from the existing body of literature? Can they provide you with a model to follow or to challenge (was their logic faulty)?

3. What *techniques* have others used to explore this and related questions? How have researchers drawn conclusions from these procedures? Past research can provide a prototype for your method, or even a target for your question: Has the research been *limited* to a single technique (e.g., naturalistic observation)? Is there a bias inherent in the methods (e.g., paper-and-pencil tests vs. behavioral observations)? Is there reason to systematically modify aspects of the traditional procedures (e.g., test subjects individually rather than in groups)?

4. What results have emerged from past research? Where is there consensus and where is there controversy?

5. In what ways do previous findings appear to be related to research strategies?

6. How have other researchers interpreted both anticipated and unanticipated findings? Where have they seen the relationship between their research and other work in the area? What sources have they drawn upon to explain their findings?

If you keep these questions in mind, you'll not only design a better study, but you'll also write a clearer proposal.

What should you do if you find that there's very little research that's directly relevant to your topic? For example, perhaps no one has actually examined the effects of music on the ability to concentrate. If this is the case, look for research in related areas. Has anyone examined the effects of variations in noise on concentration? There are advantages and disadvantages to developing research within a new area. If very little has been done on the subject, you've got a lot of room for posing questions, but you also have few guidelines or models for developing hypotheses and research methods. On the other hand, if there's a lot of relevant research, you have a great deal of structure for defining your question, hypotheses, and methods. But the drawback is that you need to familiarize yourself with all the literature, and then develop a new question or new way of looking at the issue. In this situation, some students feel that it's difficult to make an original contribution.

WRITING 6.3: ANALYZING THE LITERATURE. Using the techniques described in Chapter 8, identify the literature that is relevant to your experimental question. Record each source on a reference card in full APA format. After reading it through quickly, examine it carefully and systematically, taking notes on the relevant information (use the procedures explained in Chapter 8).

DRAFTING THE RESEARCH PROPOSAL

As we've said, the purpose of the psychological experiment is to test an hypothesis about the relationship between two or more variables. Precision is critical in both describing and conducting the research, since the ultimate goal is to describe, to explain, and to predict behavior. To promote *precise* and *concise* communication, the style and format for describing research have been standardized. The APA (1983) publication manual provides the standards for professional psychologists to follow. Therefore, much of the following discussion is based upon those guidelines.

Writing Style

Ironically, many of the students who are most successful with writing for other courses report the greatest difficulty adjusting to the research writing style. They find that their eloquent, rich descriptions are often inappropriate; their creative, poetic phrases are unwelcomed; their ability to pique the reader's interest or play with the reader's mood through subtle or ambiguous turns of phrases is not appreciated. So even if you're someone who has found writing easy, beware that you may be in for some frustration. Once you've worked on a couple of research papers, however, the writing style may begin to seem quite natural, especially as you recognize the way in which it complements the purpose of the paper.

1. Focus on an organized, logical, and direct presentation of ideas. The writer should not surprise the reader with jumps in logic or ambiguous phrasing.

2. Use precise, clear language. *Avoid* the use of:

colloquial expressions	e.g., she distributed **hand-outs** of the study
jargon	e.g., he **causally attributed** his behavior to fear
vague descriptors	e.g., subjects came from **deprived backgrounds**

Remember that one of your goals is to provide the kind of detail which would allow others to carry out your experiment with similar, if not identical, results.

3. Present your ideas as succinctly as possible. Length is not a strength when it comes to research proposals (or reports). The goal is to be complete but brief in your description. Therefore, substitute phrases with single words when possible, and avoid redundant words and phrases. For example:

Replace:	*With:*
She seemed to make the argument that a total of 30 subjects	She argued that 30 subjects
This study will examine whether or not it is true that music can distract you if it is unfamiliar.	This study will examine whether unfamiliar music is distracting.

4. Use an objective rather than subjective writing style. The emphasis on objectivity is important for several reasons. First, while your values may well influence your choice of research topic, your research will be credible only to the extent to which it appears unbiased. Second, the use of objective rather than subjective terms is necessary for precise communication of your ideas. Since we can't directly observe many of the concepts we consider in our research, we need to define them operationally — to identify them in objective terms, according to the way in which we manipulate or measure them. Therefore, replace a statement such as:

> Once subjects were **hungry,** they were given their experimental instructions.

with:

> After **eight hours without food,** subjects received their experimental instructions.

5. Except in unusual circumstances, the *voice* and *audience* of a research proposal and report are those of the professional psychologist. In terms of voice, this needn't mean that you have to be a bore. A persuasive but objective tone is best. To emphasize an objective approach, writers usually avoid frequent use of personal pronouns (**I, we**). In terms of audience, assume that your reader is familiar with common psychological terms but not necessarily an expert on your topic.

6. Carefully acknowledge the work of others. As we've explained, your rationale, method, and even interpretation *should* be linked to previous research and theory. Clearly document the source of each idea and procedure you borrow (see Chapter 9 for documentation).

7. Avoid language which is sexist (e.g., *mankind* has searched for a cure), or which is gender- or culture-biased (e.g., they coded *sex-appropriate* activities; subjects were from a *culturally deprived* background). Besides promoting potentially dangerous stereotypes, these terms introduce ambiguity and imprecision.

8. Be consistent and systematic in your choice of verb tenses:

a. When discussing completed research use the past tense.

Incorrect: Klein (1979) demonstrates similar results.
Correct: Klein (1979) demonstrated similar results.

b. Use the present perfect tense when referring to actions in the past that are not linked to one specific time.

Incorrect: Many researchers found similar effects.
Correct: Many researchers have found similar effects.

c. Similarly, use the present perfect tense when referring to actions that began in the past but continue to the present.

Incorrect: Since its publication, the book raised great controversy.
Correct: Since its publication, the book has raised great controversy.

d. Use the future tense when discussing proposed methodology and analyses and expected results and interpretations.

Correct: Subjects will complete three tasks.
Correct: Paired-comparisons will be used.
Correct: Greater recall will indicate that the memory strategy can be acquired with minimal training.

Format

The format we describe for the research proposal is based upon the APA (1983) format for a research report, since the APA establishes the most commonly adopted publication standards for psychological research. Although there is no single, uniformly accepted format for proposals, they are generally organized in the following way:

- **Title page**
- **Abstract** (not always required)
- **Introduction**
- **Method**
    - **Subjects**
    - **Apparatus** (and/or **Materials, Instruments**)
    - **Procedure**
    - **Data Analysis**
- **Results/Discussion** (not always required)
- **Appendixes** (if any)
- **References**
- **Tables** (if any)
- **Figures** (if any)

We'll discuss each of these sections in sequence, as they appear in the proposal. If you write each part as we deal with it, you'll have a completed proposal by the end of the chapter. You'll see that each section should build clearly and logically upon the earlier sections. But remember that once you complete a part, you haven't finished with it. Later sections will make you aware of what you've omitted from the earlier ones. In this way, writing a research proposal can sharpen your thinking about your research.

Title Page

Begin your proposal with a separate title page that includes a working title, your name and institutional affiliation (e.g., your school), a running head, and a short title and page number (in the top right corner).

Working title. The working title should be a concise, informative summary of your experiment and should identify your independent and dependent variables. For example, *Children's Social Skills* may be an interesting title for a book, but it doesn't tell us much about a study. In contrast, *Effects of Social Skills Training on Play of Second-Graders* identifies the independent variable (social skills training), the dependent variable (play), and the subjects (second-graders). Your title should be no longer than twelve to fifteen words; shorter titles are often more powerful. You can also use subtitles and/or questions to add clarity and emphasis. For example:

> Free-play of Second Graders: Effects of Social Skills Training
>
> **or:** Free-play of Second Graders: Can Social Skills Be Trained?

Type the working title, centered on the page, in uppercase and lowercase letters. If it requires more than one line, double-space between lines.

Running head. A running head is an abbreviated title of no more than fifty characters (including punctuation and spaces between words). It would be printed, for identification purposes, at the top of each page *if* your paper were published. Type the running head in *all* uppercase letters, centered at the bottom of the title page, and identify the running head as illustrated in Figure 6.1.

Short title. Above the page number on each page of the proposal (except figures), type the first two or three words of your title. This will allow the reader to identify the pages of your paper if they become separated. Note in Figure 6.1 that this short title is distinct from the running head (which appears only on the title page).

> WRITING 6.4: YOUR TITLE PAGE. In your journal, or on a piece of paper, write an informal, one-sentence description of your research proposal. Include your independent and dependent variables. Now, based on this statement, write three possibilities for a working title, experimenting with phrasing and sequencing of words. Revise one of these until it completely and accurately describes the subject of your proposal. Then construct the remainder of your title page.

Effects of Social
1

Effects of Social Skills Training
on Play of Second Graders
Beth Anne Bull
University of Vermont

Running head: EFFECTS OF SOCIAL SKILLS TRAINING ON
PLAY

Figure 6.1 *Title page in APA (1983) format*

Abstract

Not all instructors require an abstract in a research proposal; however, funding agencies usually do. Composing an abstract can be quite useful in clarifying the essence of your study for yourself and for others. The abstract allows readers to decide whether the full paper will be of interest to them. It also can serve as a preview of the study, so that the reader knows what to expect.

The abstract is a brief but comprehensive summary of your research. Therefore, it's often best to write your abstract *after* you've finished writing your proposal. It should include a statement of the problem, hypothesis to be tested, subjects and procedure to be used, and anticipated results and conclusions. When creating an abstract for a research proposal, don't write as if the study has been completed; use the *present* tense to describe your hypothesis and the *future* tense to describe your method, analyses, and expected results. Chapter 4 details the structure, format, and characteristics of a good abstract, as well as the procedures for constructing one. Follow the steps described in that chapter for abstracting an empirical report.

Here is the abstract page of the student proposal titled "Effects of Social Skills Training On Play Of Second Graders." Note that the abstract begins on a new page and includes the short title and page number (page 2) at the top right corner; the heading "Abstract" is centered on the first line.

Effects of Social
2

Abstract

This study will compare the effects of a behavioral social skills training (SST) program and an attention-placebo program on free-play behaviors. Thirty male and female second-graders will be randomly assigned to the experimental groups, which will meet one hour a week for eight weeks. Subjects' free-play behaviors will be coded during school recess periods before, immediately following, and eight weeks following the training period. Data will be analyzed with a 2 (Group) × 3 (Assessment period)

```
repeated measures ANOVA. It is hypothesized that
the SST group will show greater increases in pro-
social behaviors and decreases in antisocial behav-
ior than the attention-placebo control. Results
will be discussed in terms of the potential for
avoiding social incompetence and its long term neg-
ative outcomes.
```

WRITING 6.5: THE ABSTRACT. Follow the steps detailed in Chapter 4 for writing an abstract for an empirical report, but remember to indicate (through your choice of verb tense) that the study is proposed rather than completed. Again, we recommend that you write the abstract *after* you've completed the rest of the proposal.

Introduction

This section describes *what* you are going to study, *why*, and *what you expect to find*. It starts on a new page (page 3), which begins with the title of the paper centered at the top. Note that the heading "Introduction" is *not* used. The length of the introduction will depend upon the nature and complexity of your topic, but typically requires two to four pages.

The goal of the introduction is to prepare the reader to understand your experiment and its potential implications. Building on the APA (1983, pp. 24–25) guidelines, your task is to:

Introduce the problem. Begin with a general statement of the phenomenon you're investigating — but don't be too vague. You want to give the reader a firm sense of the nature of the problem being studied and its significance. It can be helpful to operationally define the constructs or variables of interest (i.e., define them in terms of how they are manipulated or measured).

Compare the following examples of opening paragraphs from two students' proposals on training social competence:

```
     Many researchers have examined the area of so-
cial competence. It is seen as an important skill
by researchers, educators, and parents. Given its
```

> importance, it is necessary to understand different ways in which social competence has been studied.

Unfortunately, this paragraph does not accomplish much. We've learned nothing about the focus of the experiment other than it deals with social competence, and that much we probably learned from reading the paper's title. We've been informed that social competence is important, but have no basis for understanding why, nor can we even be sure what the author means by the term. Then we're led to think about different ways in which social competence has been studied, although the real focus of this research is on social skills training.

Now read the opening paragraph of the proposal on "Effects of Social Skills Training on Play of Second-Graders":

> Social competence has been defined as "the ability to interact with others in a given social context in specific ways that are socially acceptable or valued and at the same time personally beneficial, mutually beneficial or beneficial primarily to others" (Combs & Slaby, 1977, p. 162). There has been great interest in factors influencing social competence in young children because the child's early social functioning is predictive of later behavioral adjustment (Cowen, Pederson, Babigian, Izzo, & Trost, 1973; Kohn & Rosman, 1972; Van Hasselt & Ross, 1979; Victor & Halverson, 1976; Waldrop & Halverson, 1975).

While you might not want to start the proposal with such a lengthy quote, this opening paragraph is more effective than the first example in providing a context for understanding both the problem and its significance.

Develop the background. Briefly review the research and theory that is directly relevant to your study. Carefully document your sources. As in the literature review paper (see Chapter 5), you need to organize and integrate the material. You might structure it chronologically, topically, by theoretical position, or by argument. Ideally, this section presents an original synthesis of the information, although this is admittedly an ambitious task.

One of the most common mistakes in an introduction is to list background information rather than to organize and integrate it for the reader. Consider this example from a student's paper:

> Emmerich and Shepard (1984) support Kohlberg's (1966) notion that gender constancy strengthens the development of same-sex-typed preferences. Marcus and Overton (1978) disagree with Kohlberg in that their research showed that the highest amount of same-sex preference peaks before gender constancy is attained. Urberg's (1982) research also confirms the hypothesis of Marcus and Overton. Marcus and Overton stated that once children attain gender constancy, they can afford to be flexible because they realize their gender will not change. Fagot (1985) also supports this evidence. Evidence by O'Brien and Huston (1985) supports Kohlberg, however, because it suggests that cognitive understanding of gender was an important contributor to developmental change.

This passage contains important information, but lists it in fragments. The student failed to go beyond the information given, and to integrate the material into a meaningful whole. A more useful approach would have been to organize the information according to evidence for and against Kohlberg, and then to identify the features which characterize each position.

A more integrative review is presented in this excerpt from a student's paper:

> As Luria (1965) points out, no behavior can be studied independently of the environmental conditions and context within which it develops. More specifically, development occurs as a result of the interaction of an individual with her social group and vice versa; each changes the other (Riegel, 1979). Harris (1975) views communications and dialogues between mother and child as an example of this individual/society discourse. When the child is young, the communication system. . . .

Unlike the literature review paper, the introduction to a research proposal should *not* be an exhaustive review of theory and research. Include only those references which have direct implications for your experiment; refer the reader to published literature reviews for additional background information. Omit details of previous work unless they help your reader understand your experimental question or procedure (e.g., you're examining the effects of different experimental instructions or measures). Remember, your audience is an intelligent person with a working knowledge of psychology and can turn to your references for greater elaboration.

State your purpose and rationale. Explain *what* you propose to do and *why*. What will your study contribute to the field and why is this contribution important? Your purpose and rationale should show a logical continuity with the background literature. Even if you've chosen to take a new approach to asking a question, your reasons for doing so should be clear. State how your design relates to previous studies (e.g., to what extent is it a replication); then explain how and why your design differs, if it does. Deviations should emerge from a careful consideration of the earlier work. Finally, define your experimental variables and formally state your hypothesis. Indicate what you expect to find and why. The rationale for each hypothesis should be clear and should be based on the findings of previous research and theory.

One of the most common problems in student papers is the failure to develop the rationale adequately. For example, one student proposed to examine whether males and females use different learning strategies. He included a solid review of the literature on classifications of learning strategies, but he failed to indicate whether there is a reason we should expect gender differences in the use of strategies. Moreover, why should we care if such gender differences do exist? For example, do the learning strategies vary in their effectiveness, thereby offering a tentative explanation for gender differences in intellectual performance?

The following is the completed introduction from the student research proposal on "Effects of Social Skills Training on Play of Second-Graders" that we've been considering throughout this chapter. Portions of the middle have been omitted for the sake of brevity. But note how the student introduces her subject, provides a background for understanding the experimental question and predictions, and ends with a formal statement of her hypothesis.

Effects of Social Skills Training
on Play of Second Graders

Social competence has been defined as "the ability to interact with others in a given social context in specific ways that are socially acceptable or valued and at the same time personally beneficial, mutually beneficial, or beneficial primarily to others" (Combs & Slaby, 1977, p. 162). There has been great interest in factors influencing social competence in young children because the child's early social functioning is predictive of later behavioral adjustment (e.g., Cowen, Pederson, Babigian, Izzo, & Trost, 1973; Kohn & Rosman, 1972; Van Hasselt & Ross, 1979; Victor & Halverson, 1976; Waldrop & Halverson, 1975). Cowen et al. (1973) found that a disproportionate percentage of children who were judged socially ineffective in elementary school developed some form of psychiatric difficulty over a subsequent 11–13 year follow-up. Even among preschool-aged children, social withdrawal has predicted lower academic achievement (e.g., Kohn & Rosman, 1972; Victor & Halverson, 1976) and difficulties interacting with peers (e.g., Victor & Halverson, 1976; Waldrop & Halverson, 1975) three to five years later in school.

Given the extent of the problems associated with low social competence in children, several interventions have been implemented for the prevention and/or treatment of social skills deficits. One of these, Social Skills Training (SST) has demonstrated ''potent treatment effects across a wide variety of clinical and non-clinical populations'' (Michelson, Mannarino, Stern, Figueroa, & Beck, 1983a, p. 545). SST supports Behavior Therapy strategies and stresses the development of effective social responses and improved interpersonal relationships (Hops & Greenwood, 1981). Some of the behavioral methods typically employed in this training program include: instructions, modelling, rehearsal, feedback, role-playing, role-reversal, shaping, and social reinforcement (Michelson et al., 1983a).

In the past, SST has yielded significant treatment effects for children labelled unassertive, highly aggressive, socially maladjusted, academically deficient, disruptive, and peer-rejected. Bornstein, Bellack, and Hersen (1977) found that a nine-session SST intervention led to considerable improvement in specific verbal and non-verbal components of assertiveness, as well as overall assertiveness. Furthermore, treatment effects were consistent at a one-month follow-up. . . .

Michelson et al. (1983a) described various assessment tools that have been used to evaluate social skills training programs. These include self-report measures such as the Piers-Harris Children's Self-Concept Scale; teacher- or parent-rating scales, such as the Behavior Problem Checklist (BPC); and peer sociometric forms, such as the Roster-and-Rating Sociometric Questionnaires. Other assessment tools include behavioral interviews (Campbell & Yarrow, 1961, as cited in Van Hasselt et al., 1979), and to a limited extent, behavioral observations (e.g., Bornstein et al., 1977; Dunlop, Stoneman, & Cantrell, 1980).

In fact, the assessment tool that appears to be potentially most informative is the behavioral observation technique. According to Cairns and Green (1979, p. 224):

> For the purposes of understanding the mechanisms of social patterns (how they are maintained and changed and how new patterns are brought into the repertoire of individuals and groups), there can be no substitute for the direct analysis of the activities to be explained.

Furthermore. . . . But despite the support for the behavioral observation method, it is rarely used, perhaps because of its time-demanding nature and its difficulty in detecting low occurrence behaviors. Its advantages, however, seem to outweigh these disadvantages.

A second limitation of previous evaluations of SST programs is that no-treatment control groups, rather than attention-placebo groups, have been used for comparison (Coie & Krehbiel, 1984). The attention-placebo group differs from a no-treatment control group in that. . . .

In an attempt to overcome the design and measurement limitations of the previous research, this study will compare changes in the free-play behaviors of children who have participated in an eight-week SST program with those of an attention-placebo group. It is hypothesized that, compared to the attention-placebo control, the SST group will show significantly more improvement in socially competent behavior from pre-intervention to post-intervention, and from post-intervention to an eight-week follow-up assessment. Specifically, the SST group will show greater increases in prosocial behavior and greater decreases in aggressive/antisocial behavior than the control group.

Method

Subjects

Subjects will be. . . .

WRITING 6.6: YOUR INTRODUCTION. Make a rough outline of an introduction for your proposal: Introduce the problem, develop the background, and state the purpose and rationale for your study. Then assemble your notes on the background literature and write a first draft. Don't worry about spelling and details of phrasing; just get the main ideas down on paper. Revise with emphasis on organization — build in a logical sequence from your opening paragraph to the final statement of your hypothesis. Then consider style, phrasing, grammar, and punctuation with the goal of concise, accurate communication. Ask a friend to read the draft and use the feedback for further revision. Compare the structure of your introduction with the models we presented in this chapter. Are you presenting the material in an integrated and precise manner?

Method

The method section does *not* begin on a new page; rather the heading "Method" is centered on a new line immediately following the introduction. (Note that only the first letter of the heading is capitalized.)

Your introduction explained what you want to examine and why. Your method section should explain *how* you plan to conduct your research. The method should be described in enough detail to allow an experienced investigator to conduct your experiment. You may not have worked out all the details of the experiment, but be as precise as possible. On the other hand, don't include information that isn't essential; it will only distract the reader.

There's good reason to consider practicalities when designing your method, even if you know you'll never have to conduct the experiment. Devising a feasible study is an important contribution to the field. Even if you wouldn't conduct it, someone else might. More importantly, designing a workable study requires a sensitivity to the real constraints on psychological research (time, money, ethical considerations, etc.). Therefore, writing such a proposal helps you to develop and demonstrate more sophisticated analytical and research skills.

The method section includes subsections on **Subjects, Apparatus** (and/or **Materials, Instruments**), and **Procedure.** You are also usually expected to include a subsection on **Data Analysis.** You may decide that you should include additional subsections as well. For example, if you are planning to use distinct groups of experimenters or experimental confederates, you may find it useful to describe them in a separate section. If your experimental methods are quite complex, you may want to begin your Method section with a subsection titled "Overview." The decision is yours, but don't get carried away. Most information which does not describe subjects, apparatus, or analyses can be included in the procedure subsection. Each of the subsections immediately follows the one before (no new page) and begins with an underlined heading typed flush on the left margin (in uppercase and lowercase letters). The first sentence of each subsection starts a new paragraph (see the "Subjects" example below).

Subjects. The description of subjects should address three questions: Who will participate in the study? How many participants will there be? How will they be selected? (APA, 1983, p. 26). Explain the procedures you will use to select and assign subjects, as well as any agreements or compensation that will be made (e.g., money, or points toward a course grade). Identify important characteristics of your participants (age, gender) and other criteria for participating in your study such as institutional affiliation, geographic location, educational level, etc.). Be certain to specify characteristics which distinguish subjects in different experimental groups (e.g., "The attention group will be drawn from a neighboring junior college."). Also indicate the procedures you will use to obtain informed consent from your participants. When your subjects are animals, indicate their genus, species, strain number, and supplier, if possible, and any details regarding their treatment, housing, and feeding which might be relevant.

Here is the subsection on subjects from the social skills training proposal:

Method

Subjects

Subjects will be drawn from a population of 46 second-graders (age 7–8 years) in an elementary school in Burlington, VT. With consent of school personnel, descriptions of the study will be sent to each child's parents. Sixteen male and sixteen female participants will be randomly selected from those families that provide written parental and child consent. Children identified by their teachers as having physical or mental disabilities (IQ below 80) will not be included in the study.

Apparatus. The apparatus subsection presents a brief description of the apparatus, materials, or instruments, and their intended function. Don't elaborate upon common or standard items such as stopwatches or tape recorders unless they have unique characteristics important to the study. Rather than including lengthy descriptions, you can use a photograph or drawing to illustrate custom-made equipment. Identify specialized equipment by indicating the manufacturer and model number. If more appropriate, label this subsection "Materials" or "Instruments" instead of "Apparatus"; in some cases, you'll need all three subsections. Consider these examples from the student proposal on social skills training:

Apparatus

Videotape recordings will be made with a standard, portable, ½ inch, VHS video-recorder (JVC #2200). The video-camera, equipped with a tripod and zoom lens, will be positioned approximately 35 feet from the play area.

The play area will be a 40 × 40 foot section of an outdoor, elementary school playground, and will include standard playground equipment as illustrated in Figure 1.

Insert Figure 1 about here

Instruments

Dunlop et al.'s (1980) behavioral coding instrument will be used to record children's play behaviors. This instrument records four major categories of behaviors: (a) Solitary Activity; (b) Direct Interaction/Dominant; (c) Direct Interaction/Cooperative; and (d) Adult-Child Interaction. These four categories are composed of a total of 27

```
mutually exclusive codable behaviors, each opera-
tionally defined (see Table 1).

                 Insert Table 1 about here

The observer will use a time sampling technique,
recording the child's behavior at each 20-second
interval.

Materials

     Social skills training programs developed by
Jackson et al. (1984) and McGinnis et al. (1984)
will be combined to generate a series of nine one-
hour training sessions. All materials from each of
these training packages will be distributed to par-
ticipants. The resulting program will involve the
following behavioral methods: (a) modelling, (b)
positive reinforcement, (c) coaching and practice,
(d) behavioral rehearsal, and (e) feedback (see Ap-
pendix A for a sample lesson).
```

Procedure. This subsection provides a step-by-step account of how you will conduct the study. Include (although not necessarily in this order):

- instructions to the (human) subjects; these should be summarized or paraphrased unless they are unique and/or an important part of the experimental manipulation, in which case you should present them verbatim
- assignment of subjects to experimental groups
- manipulation of experimental variables
- techniques for controlling extraneous variables (e.g., randomization, counterbalancing, and special efforts to maintain consistent treatment across conditions)
- the order in which subjects will receive multiple trials or experimental conditions
- the method for measuring dependent variables (and sequence, if multiple measures are to be used)
- procedures for debriefing human subjects.

Address these points in a logical sequence. You might start by describing the procedure in the order in which it will be executed. Elaborate on each detail of the methodological design as it is introduced in your paper. Use simple, concise language. Remember that your method should be sufficiently clear and detailed to enable another experimenter to conduct your study.

Writing the procedure section can lead to major revelations about the inadequacies of your experimental design. You start talking to yourself, "Wait a minute — how can I give the subjects both treatments without biasing their thinking?" or "Now that I've described each treatment and assessment, this procedure seems much too long." Don't feel you've failed if you suddenly recognize that your original plans for your procedure won't work. This is one reason that researchers write research proposals — to discover and solve their methodological problems. It's better to learn what's wrong at the proposal stage than to wait until you're in the midst of your experiment. The following is an excerpt from the procedure section of "Effects of Social Skills Training on Play of Second Graders":

Procedure

This study will be part of a larger doctoral thesis project that has already been approved by the University of Vermont Committee on Human Experimentation. Permission to conduct the study will be obtained from the principal and teachers of the participating elementary school. Informed consent will be obtained from the participating students and their parents.

Children will be administered the Roster-and-Rating Sociometric Questionnaire (Michelson et al., 1983a) individually, in a corner of the classroom. On the basis of their scores, subjects will be ranked from most to least popular. Then each subject will be assigned to one of two behavioral social skills training groups or one of two attention-placebo control groups (n=8 in each of the four groups). Subject assignment will be conducted in a way so that equal numbers of boys and girls at high, medium, and low levels of social skills are placed in each group.

Each group will have eight weekly one-hour meetings, conducted during class time. A different trainer will be in charge of each group; the trainers will be blind to the experimental hypothesis.

The Dunlop (1980) behavioral observations of children's free play behavior will be conducted by observers who are blind to the children's treatment condition. Observations will be made one week before, one week after, and eight weeks following the group interventions. Each child will be observed for ten minutes on each of two consecutive days during an unstructured, outdoor, morning recess period.

At the end of the study, subjects' parents will be sent a brief summary of the experimental findings and will have the opportunity to discuss the study further with the experimenter. Parents of children in the attention-placebo group will also have the option to enroll their children in a subsequent social skills training group at the school.

Data Analysis. This section describes how your data will be scored and the statistical tests you will use to analyze them. But beware. Simply naming your statistical test is not sufficient. You need to indicate the specific variables that will be involved in the analysis. For example, rather than saying, "Results will be analyzed with Pearson Product-Moment Correlations," explain that "the relationship between amount of caffeine consumed and speed of running the maze will be analyzed using Pearson Product-Moment Correlations." The following is the data analysis section from the proposal on social skills training:

Data Analysis

Four behavioral summary scores will be calculated for each child, by summing the child's total number of behaviors in each of the following categories: (a) Solitary Activity, (b) Direct Interaction/Dominant; (c) Direct Interaction/Cooperative; and (d) Adult-Child Interaction. A separate Group (Treatment vs. Control) × Assessment (Pretest, Posttest, Follow-up) analysis of variance will be used to examine experimental effects on each of the four types of behavior.

You may find that you're asked to write research proposals before you have been trained in statistical analyses. That really isn't a problem. Even if you can't propose a specific statistical test, you should have a sense of the *type* of comparison you'll need. For example, one of our freshmen wrote that he would "compare the average number of words remembered by subjects in the experimental vs. the control group." That's a fairly clear statement of the nature of the analysis which needs to be done.

The data analysis section is a very important part of your proposal and your thinking, even if you're not specifying particular statistical tests. The most carefully designed experimental procedure is worthless unless you know how to use the data to draw meaningful conclusions.

> WRITING 6.7: YOUR METHOD. Make a rough outline of your Method section. Be certain to include subsections on Subjects, Apparatus (and/or Materials, Instruments), Procedures, and Data Analysis. Then organize your notes according to your outline. As you begin to draft your Method, don't be concerned with the details of spelling and phrasing. First, get all the critical information down on paper. Then revise, with precision and clarity. Check to see that you've provided enough detail to enable another researcher to conduct your study.

Results/Discussion

The Results/Discussion section does *not* begin a new page; the heading "Results/Discussion" (typed in uppercase and lowercase letters) is centered on a new line immediately following the Method section.

Because you're only proposing your study, you don't actually have results. But a Results/Discussion section is sometimes included to describe the results you expect to find, and the way in which you'll interpret the findings. If the introduction to your proposal is extraordinarily clear and complete, the results/discussion section may seem redundant. But writing this section helps you to check on the logic and coherence of your entire proposal, and to consider the relationship among your hypotheses, method, and analyses.

1. Begin this section by describing the pattern of results that would confirm your hypothesis. This will lead you to ask an important question: Is your research design responsive to your hypothesis?

2. Explain the specific implications of the findings you anticipate; that is, describe the way in which the findings would address the experimental question. (Will your data allow you to reach the kinds of conclusions you hope to reach?) You may have designed your study to test competing hypotheses. If so, describe the alternative patterns of data suggested by these hypotheses, and the interpretations of each.

3. Explain the general significance that your findings could have for the larger field of study. That is, reconsider the broad context of your research question, which you have introduced in the opening paragraph of your proposal.

Here is the Results/Discussion section from the proposal on the effects of social skills training:

Results/Discussion

A Group x Assessment interaction is predicted: It is expected that children in the social skills training groups will show greater increases in prosocial behaviors and decreases in antisocial behaviors than children in the attention-placebo groups. Tests of simple effects should reveal significant effects between groups at both posttest and followup assessment periods, indicating that the intervention has both immediate and long term effects on the play behaviors of the children. This finding would support the notion that a fairly brief program of social skills training can have important effects on the ways in which children play with one another in naturalistic settings.

If the training effects are found at posttest but not at followup, it would suggest that the beneficial effects of the intervention are short lasting. If the effects are found at followup but not at posttest, it might be that the benefits of social skills training take time to be realized but can continue to grow (following training) even in the absence of continued training. Both of these findings would have important implications for deciding when to evaluate training studies.

In summary, it is predicted that this study will confirm that social competence in naturalistic settings can be enhanced by behavioral training in social skills. Given the relationship between social competence (and particularly peer relationships) and subsequent healthy development, any program which can improve this competence may be an important tool for improving psychological functioning in general.

WRITING 6.8: YOUR RESULTS/DISCUSSION. Outline and draft your Results/Discussion section according to the steps described: Present the pattern of results that would confirm your hypothesis, the specific implications of the findings you anticipate, and the general significance of your expected findings for the larger field of study. Make certain that your Results/Discussion section is logically connected to your Introduction and Method sections.

A NOTE ON TABLES, FIGURES, and APPENDIXES: It's possible that you'll want to include tables, figures, or appendixes in your proposal. However, they are more commonly used when writing a research report. Therefore, the discussion of their format, function, and placement is detailed in Chapter 7, The Research Report. Turn to those sections for further information, if relevant to your proposal.

Revising

If you've completed each of the writing assignments in this chapter, you should have a completed draft of your research proposal. It's likely that you've already made notes to revise earlier portions of your draft as you worked out details in later sections of the proposal. Writing a research proposal is a problem-solving activity, as we've stressed. The sections of the proposal are not independent, but rather are interrelated. Therefore:

1. Begin the revision process by considering the proposal as a whole, checking for continuity and coherence in logic.

2. Once you feel confident that you've maintained a consistent theme and direction from beginning to end, check to be sure that each individual section is accurate and complete.

3. Finally, refine grammar, word choice, and spelling, to add precision and clarity to your paragraphs and sentences.

As we've suggested in earlier chapters, ask one or two classmates to read your draft. They can give you a sense of whether you've got a clear and logical presentation. If your classmates find your proposal confusing, it's likely that an instructor or funding agency will also. So consider their feedback carefully as you revise your paper.

Keep in mind that it's difficult to take a fresh look at your thinking/writing immediately after you've created it. You know too well what you wanted to say. And whether you feel generally positive or negative about what you've produced, you're still too close to it to take an objective view. Therefore, put your proposal aside for a few days, or at least a few hours. You can't be sure whether it'll look better or worse after getting away from it, but it's likely it will look different. Remember that this technique can serve you well at any point in drafting your paper. If you get stuck on some part and the words won't come, get away and return to it later.

WRITING 6.10: REVISING YOUR RESEARCH PROPOSAL. Assemble the sections of the proposal which you've drafted, and read the whole proposal. Revise, using the sequence described above. Exchange your paper with classmates and incorporate their feedback into your revisions. Be sure to put your paper aside for some time during the revision process.

References

This section begins a new page, with the heading "References" centered at the top (in uppercase and lowercase letters). List the full documentation for each source that you cited in your proposal, using APA (1983) format (see Chapter 9). Unless your instructor says otherwise, include only the references you've cited. The reference list is not assumed to demonstrate how much you've read; it serves to document your proposal. Don't compile your reference list until after you've completed (but not typed) the *final* draft of your proposal, since you may add and delete citations during your revisions. If you recorded each reference in APA format on a separate 3″ × 5″ card when you previewed the literature, constructing your reference list will be relatively easy. Just assemble the appropriate cards and order them according to APA guidelines (Chapter 9).

WRITING 6.11: YOUR REFERENCE LIST. Carefully go through your paper, page by page, and pull the reference card for each source you've cited. As you do, check to see that you've been consistent with spelling and publication dates, and that you've used **et al.** when you've repeated a citation of a work by three or more authors (see Chapter 9). Alphabetize your references according to APA guidelines. You should now have a finished proposal.

TYPING YOUR MANUSCRIPT

As with any paper, a sloppy proposal suggests sloppy thinking. In addition, small typographical errors can sometimes lead to significant distortions in meaning. So don't underestimate the importance of typing your paper carefully. Even if you've hired a professional typist, proofread your paper. Then get your roommate or a classmate to do it as well; he or she will often catch errors you simply overlooked. It's best to proofread after you've been away from the paper for a while. Otherwise, you'll read your words as you composed them rather than as they are typed. Then make a photocopy of your paper to keep on hand in case the original becomes lost or misplaced.

CHECKLIST FOR THE RESEARCH PROPOSAL

1. Title Page (page 1)

Is your title informative and accurate? Does it indicate your independent and dependent variables?

Does your title page follow the format shown on page 113, or requested by your instructor?

2. Abstract (page 2)

Is the abstract 150 words or less?

Does your abstract comprehensively summarize the problem, subjects, procedures, and expected results and conclusions?

3. Introduction (begins on page 3 with title of paper on the first line)

Do you clearly describe (a) the problem, (b) the relevant background literature, (c) the rationale for your specific experimental design, and (d) your formal hypothesis (or hypotheses)?

4. Method (immediately follows Introduction)

Do you describe your subjects, apparatus, instruments, materials, and procedures in adequate detail?

Do you specify your method of data analysis (if one will be used)?

5. Results/Discussion (immediately follows Method)

Do you describe the pattern of results that would confirm your hypothesis?

Do you explain why the study is important?

Do you explain the significance of the project for the larger field of study?

6. References (begins a new page)

Have you listed every reference you cited in your proposal, and only those sources?

Are your references in full APA documentation style and arranged in alphabetical order?

Have you actually read all the references you list?

Overall Considerations:

Have you included all appropriate citations in the text of your proposal?

Have you used APA format (or the format requested by your instructor) for ordering and presenting information *throughout* your proposal?

Do the sections of your proposal fit together in a coherent whole?

HAVE YOU PROOFREAD YOUR FINAL TYPED DRAFT?

Have you photocopied your paper?

[7] *The Research Report*

PREVIEW:

We live in a world shaped by researchers. Most everything around you — from the weight of the hamburger you ate at MacDonald's to the number of public parks in your city — was analyzed, calculated, and discussed in some manner before becoming accessible to you. Research can help sell products and images (which is how Madison Avenue uses it); it can also revolutionize the way we think and behave. But whether research is used to sustain current beliefs or to support radical changes, its information is only as good as the way in which it's communicated to others. In psychology, the research report is the primary means for this communication.

Of course, a good research report does much more than present experimental results. In fact, in many reports, the synthesis of background literature, the research strategy, and the new questions which emerge are more important than the experimental findings themselves. So let us emphasize that you needn't have confirmed your hypothesis in order to develop an impressive research report. Actually, once you've carefully designed your study, you have little control over whether or not you get positive results — that's nature you're testing. You are responsible, however, for creating a meaningful synthesis of information which develops logically into a hypothesis, procedure, analysis, and interpretation of results.

Like it or not, the quality of your written report will influence the way others judge the quality of your research. If your report is confusing or imprecise, your research will also appear sloppy. Writing an effective report is part of being a good researcher. And writing a research report also helps you to *become* a good researcher. You're forced to examine your work critically and consider its full implications — tasks which often get put aside when preoccupied with conducting your study. And learning to write research reports also teaches you how to read them with an eye toward the characteristics that determine their scientific quality.

COMPOSING THE RESEARCH REPORT

The outline for a research report looks like this:

- **Title page**
- **Abstract**
- **Introduction**
- **Method**
  - **Subjects**
  - **Apparatus** (if necessary)
  - **Materials** (if necessary)
  - **Procedure**
  - **Data Analysis** (if necessary)
- **Results**
- **Discussion**
- **References**

Appendixes (if any)

Author Notes (if any)

Footnotes (if any)

Tables (if any)

Figures (if any)

As indicated, some of the subsections of the Method are optional. Include them when the information is lengthy or complex, or when an instructor specifically requests them. Otherwise, the material can be incorporated into other subsections (typically the Procedure).

Using this outline for a model, you're ready to think about drafting your research report. Where do you begin? You already should have two valuable sources on hand which will make your job easier and more productive: your research proposal and your laboratory journal.

Using Your Research Proposal

If you followed Chapter 6 in writing a proposal for your research, you've got a significant start on your report already. If you haven't done a proposal, you'll need to turn to Chapter 6 and review the steps described. As you may have noticed, the report includes the same sections as the proposal, with the addition of complete and separate Results and Discussion sections replacing the proposal's combined Results/Discussion. But writing a research report is not as simple as tacking the Results and Discussion to your proposal because, as you know, nothing in life turns out exactly as you expect — including research!

No matter how carefully you design your study, some of the details are likely to change as you conduct it. For example, you may find that you have to alter your procedures for recruiting subjects. Subjects may fail to complete your project for a variety of reasons. Or you may find that you have to change your experimental manipulation because your original plan is ineffective or impractical. Therefore, writing a research report typically involves modifying your proposal to some degree.

In addition to the details, the general orientation of your experimental question may shift. For example, your most striking finding may not involve your major hypothesis, but rather the dramatic differences in subject performance from trial to trial or task to task. In this case, you might change your introduction so that the reader will be prepared to follow your discussion of these findings. In a moment we'll elaborate upon the specific modifications necessary when going from your research proposal to your report.

Using a Lab Journal

Maintaining a lab journal (introduced in Chapter 2) makes the drafting process more simple and productive. As you conduct your research, you keep your journal by your side. You note the time and date of each experimental session, and record precisely what you do and when (e.g., "I began to give the experimental instructions as we were walking to the observation room."). This makes you more conscientious about conforming to your planned procedure and more aware of important deviations that you adopt (and when you begin to adopt them). You note questions about your procedure, data coding, subjects' reactions, etc. (e.g., "I wonder if my subjects feel anxious being observed?"). You record casual thoughts and observation (e.g., "My subjects looked confused after the last set of instructions" or "These two animals got jumpy after the noise in the hallway"). Later in this chapter you'll see that these comments can be tremendously helpful when you're writing the Discussion section of your report, and they're difficult to reconstruct once you're removed from the experimental setting. Your journal should include the procedures and results of your data analyses, including your computer printouts. And the journal is a place to translate the meaning of your statistical tests, interpret your findings, and think about the implications of your research.

WRITING STYLE AND FORMAT

The standards for the style and format of research reports are established in the APA (1983) publication manual. We used these standards as the basis for our detailed discussion of style and format of a research proposal. As we've already addressed these features in Chapter 6, we won't repeat them here. **Use Chapter 6, The Research Proposal, as the basis for your research report as well.** In the remainder of this chapter we will stress those modifications and additions to the proposal which are necessary for completing a research report.

Style

Use the writing style precisely as detailed in Chapter 6; however, use verb tenses which reflect the fact that your study is now completed. Use the past tense to present your hypothesis, method, and results. For example:

> There were two hypotheses.
>
> Subjects were assigned . . . .
>
> The correlations revealed . . . .

Use the present tense to *discuss* your results and to present your conclusions. For example:

> The strong correlations suggest that there may be . . . .
>
> In conclusion, training is an effective means for . . . .

Format

As we've explained, the major difference between the research proposal and report is that the report requires a full presentation of the experimental results and their interpretation. However, we emphasized that you'll probably need to modify the other sections of your proposal as well, before incorporating them into your report. In considering each section of the research report sequentially, we'll emphasize the issues you need to consider in developing your report beyond your proposal and lab journal.

Title Page

Now that you've completed your research, rewrite your working title to describe your study accurately and concisely. Consider whether the focus of your findings shifted from what you had originally anticipated. Be as informative as you can; it's helpful to indicate your independent and dependent variables. If you modify your title, you'll also have to change your short title (typed on the top right corner of each page), and you'll probably want to alter your running head as well.

Abstract

You may or may not have included an abstract in your research proposal, but every research report *must* have one. Since the abstract should be a brief, comprehensive summary of your entire experiment, we suggest that you write the abstract last, after you've drafted the full report. Although you may have included an abstract in your proposal, it's often best to start from scratch in drafting a new one. The abstract should truly reflect the content of your report, much of which has been added or modified since the proposal. Thus you'll need to add a statement of your results, conclusions, and implications. You'll also need to consider ways in which the focus of your research has shifted. Chapter 4 details the structure, format, and characteristics of a good abstract, and explains how to construct one. Follow the procedures described for abstracting an **empirical report.**

Introduction

The introduction may remain relatively unchanged from that of your proposal. However, once you've collected your experimental results and considered their interpretation and implications, you'll need to modify your introduction so that it will prepare the reader for subsequent results and discussion. It's likely that you'll decide on even further changes once you actually draft your Results and Discussion sections. You might find that you need to read and incorporate information from new, related background areas in order to make sense of your results. Or that certain issues you originally discussed in great detail no longer seem to warrant such emphasis. As you revise your introduction, be certain that references to your hypothesis and procedure are stated in the past tense (e.g., "It was hypothesized that," or "This study examined").

Method

The method section of your proposal will probably require considerable revision before it's appropriate for your report. And as we've said, your lab journal can be extremely important in this.

Subjects. You'll need to modify your original description of subjects to reflect accurately what happened in your study. What procedures for subject recruitment were actually necessary? How many subjects participated in the project? How many subjects failed to complete the study and for what reasons? Describe the actual characteristics of the subjects who participated, and specify important characteristics of those who dropped out.

Apparatus, Materials, and **Instruments.** The apparatus, materials, and/or instruments you used in your experiment may be different from those you originally proposed. When beginning an experiment, you often create modifications to improve your study. As you conduct your research you might also discover that you have inadvertently arranged your apparatus or developed your materials differently from how you had planned. These issues should be recorded in your lab journal and incorporated in your report.

Procedure. In the procedure section, you'll need to record exactly what you did in your research and the sequence in which you did it. Whether intentional or not, you rarely follow your original design exactly as planned. For example, you might shorten your procedure if your subjects appear to tire, or you might change the sequence of administering your measures for practical reasons. Your lab journal will be particularly important in guiding this section of your draft. Include your procedures for checking your experimental manipulation (if any) and for debriefing your subjects (if humans were involved).

Data Analysis. You should have presented a reasonable data analysis plan in your proposal. But often, the specific analyses you use must be modified in response to the data you collect. For example, if your preliminary analyses reveal that female and male subjects responded similarly in your study, you could combine their data in further analyses. But if male and female subjects responded differently, you need to analyze their data separately, maintaining gender as an independent variable. Again, all of the information necessary for this section should have been recorded in your lab journal.

WRITING 7.1: YOUR TITLE PAGE, INTRODUCTION, AND METHOD. If you haven't already done so, draft your title page, introduction, and method sections using the steps described here and in Chapter 6. Adapt information from your research proposal and your lab journal where appropriate. Don't be concerned with polishing your drafts at this time. You'll need to revise them further once you've drafted your Results and Discussion sections.

Results

Your research proposal included a Results/Discussion section which only speculated on potential findings and interpretations. In contrast, the research report must include a fully developed Results section, separate from the Discussion which follows.

The Results section details the findings of your experiment, without discussing their importance or implications. It immediately follows the Method section, *not* on a new page. The heading "Results" (typed in uppercase and lowercase letters) should be centered on the first line. Present your results clearly and directly, using simple, precise statements. The following guidelines should help you to deal with both the content and organization of this material.

1. Throughout this section, as you address each of your results, *first* present a brief statement of your main finding (without elaborating on your statistical analyses); *then* give details of your data and analyses in order to justify your statement. For example:

Results

Comparisons between the intervention, attention-placebo, and control groups showed that training improved accuracy. A one-way analysis of variance on mean number of correct responses indicated a significant difference between group means, $F(2,48)=3.41$, $p < .05$. Unplanned comparisons revealed that the mean score of the intervention group (22.4) was significantly higher than that of the control group (14.2), $F(2,48)=5.49$, $p < .01$; the mean of the attention-placebo group (18.9) did not differ from the others, $F(2,48)=1.01$, $p > .05$.

Don't discuss your findings here; that's left for the next section of the report.

2. Include **descriptive** statistics (i.e., those that summarize your data) such as means, medians, quartile ranges, or frequency distributions. But don't overwhelm the reader; include only that information which is directly relevant to understanding the results.

3. If appropriate (and if you've had the training to do so), describe **inferential** statistics, that is, those that test the likelihood that your findings were due to chance, for example, F, t, and r values. When you do, be certain to indicate the magnitude or value of the test, the degrees of freedom (in parentheses), the probability level, and the direction of the effect. The earlier example illustrates standard APA format for reporting statistical tests of significance. Be quite specific when referring to statistical tests. It is not enough to say that, "A correlational analysis revealed. . . ." You need to specify that, for example, "A Pearson Product-Moment Correlation Analysis revealed. . . ."

If you've been trained in inferential statistics and use them in your report, avoid these common mistakes:

a. Refer to significant **effects,** *not* significant **results.** The latter suggests that a finding was important. Your statistical test reveals the likelihood that your finding was due to chance. Whether or not it is an important finding is a matter for you to decide.
b. When statistical tests do not reach critical values, describe them as **nonsignificant,** or state that **no significant differences** were found, rather than use the term **insignificant.** Again, the latter suggests a reference to importance instead of statistical probability.
c. Be certain to describe the **direction** of the differences which are found.

Instead of:	There was a significant difference between the mean anxiety scores of Group A and Group B.
Report:	The mean anxiety score for Group A was significantly higher than that for Group B.

d. Ask your instructor whether you should report all values of your statistical tests (F's, t's, r's, etc.), whether significant or not. This requirement varies from course to course.

4. Do *not* include raw data or individual scores unless you have a single-subject design, or you want to illustrate a particular point about those scores (e.g., that group data hide an important individual pattern).

5. Mention *all analyses,* even if their results were not statistically significant, or contradicted your predictions. On the other hand, don't elaborate on every nonsignificant test; emphasize the results that are meaningful and important. And remember that your audience is presumed to be knowledgeable about statistics; therefore, you don't need to explain the basics (e.g., the assumptions of common statistical tests).

6. Present your findings in a clear, logical sequence.

a. Begin the results section with any preliminary analyses that served as a basis for checking your manipulations, regrouping your data, or modifying your analyses. For example:

> Preliminary <u>t</u>-tests revealed no differences between male and female performance within treatments, <u>t</u>(24) = 0.14, <u>p</u> > .05. Therefore, data for males and females were combined for subsequent analyses.

b. Report your major analyses in the sequence in which you presented your predictions. Begin with your primary hypothesis, then refer to your secondary hypotheses (if any), then report the findings of exploratory analyses. This organization of your results is important for maintaining a focus on your hypotheses.

7. Use **Tables** and **Figures** when helpful. Tables and figures can be referred to anywhere in a research report, but they are often part of the Results or Method sections. Tables list and classify information (typically data). Figures are diagrams, graphs, or illustrations. Both can be useful when you are describing data from several dependent variables, a complex experimental design (e.g., a factorial), or extensive analyses. For example, consider the following presentation of information:

> The mean numbers of words recalled by the children who received the intervention were 12.8, 14.9, and 16.7 for the 5-, 7-, and 9-year-olds, respectively. The mean numbers of words recalled by the

children in the attention-placebo group were 8.1, 12.9, and 16.8 for the 5-, 7-, and 9-year-olds, respectively. The mean numbers of words recalled by the children in the no-treatment control group were 8.8, 13.1, and 16.5 for the 5-, 7-, and 9-year-olds, respectively.

Now here's the same information presented in a table:

Table 3. Mean Numbers of Words Recalled as a Function of Age and Treatment

	Age (in years)[a]		
Treatment	5	7	9
Intervention	12.8	14.9	16.7
Attention-placebo	8.1[b]	12.9	16.8
No-treatment	8.8	13.1	16.5

Note. Maximum score possible = 20. Cell *n*'s = 22.
[a]Age was calculated using birth date, plus or minus six months. [b]Two subjects in this group did not complete the assessment in the designated time limit.

As you can see, a table can have several advantages over a textual presentation of data. It can (a) organize the information for the reader, (b) present a large amount of information concisely, (c) avoid repetition of words, and (d) add general clarity to the information. On the other hand, there are instances in which it is simpler and more concise to state the findings in words. Never use a table or figure unless there is a good reason for doing so.

The use and format of tables and figures is detailed in the APA manual (1983, pp. 83–105). The following guidelines and format descriptions are based on that information:

1. Tables and figures are meant to supplement the text, and should not duplicate information presented in the text or in another table or figure.

2. Tables and figures should be understandable by themselves based on their titles, headings, and notes (which will be discussed shortly).

3. Tables and figures should not be seen as replacements for verbal descriptions of important findings. Never include a table or figure without referring to it in your text. You can make this reference in a couple of ways:

> The cell means are presented in Table 2.
>
> There was great variation in cell size across treatments (see Table 4).

Moreover, you must use your text to guide the reader through an understanding of the table or figure, without specifying (i.e., duplicating) the details of the information. For example, in reference to Table 3, do not simply state:

> The mean numbers of words recalled by each age group in the three treatment conditions are presented in Table 3. The Age × Treatment interaction was significant.

Instead, write:

> The mean numbers of words recalled at each age in each treatment condition are presented in Table 3. Note that treatment effects diminished with age. A 3 × 3 analysis of variance (Age × Treatment) revealed a significant interaction. . . .

4. If you are using APA (1983) format, each table should be typed on a separate page. Like all other pages in your report (except figures), type the short title and page number flush right at the top of the page. Use the following guidelines for the various parts of a table:

Table number. Tables are numbered in arabic numerals (i.e., 1, 2, etc.) in the order in which they are referred to in your text. They are numbered independently of figures (you might have Tables 1 through 3 and Figures 1 and 2). As illustrated in our earlier example, the table number is typed flush left on the first line, in uppercase and lowercase letters.

Descriptive title. Include a brief, explanatory title for your table. Be as clear and precise as possible. Remember that the table should be understandable without reference to the text. When appropriate, include the relationship between the independent and dependent variables. Be certain to explain what the data in your table represent (e.g., mean numbers of problems solved, or Pearson Product-Moment correlation coefficients).

Headings. Headings are used to organize the information you present. They must be clear and precise to allow accurate interpretation. Make your headings as brief as possible, but don't sacrifice clarity. You can use abbreviations for headings as long as they are commonly known (e.g., IQ), or you can define them in a table note (described below). If you find yourself repeating portions of headings, try using a **decked heading,** where one heading is stacked on top of another. In the earlier example, Table 3, we used a decked heading to present age groups:

Decked Heading:

Age (in years)		
5	7	9

Instead of:

5 years old	7 years old	9 years old

Body. The body of your table will usually consist of data. Use a consistent unit of measurement throughout the table, and, if possible, a consistent degree of precision (e.g., present all data to two decimal places). Don't include information which can be calculated easily from other data in the table. For example, if you present the number of correct responses on twenty trials, you shouldn't then present the number of incorrect responses. Some tables consist of words rather than numbers. For example, you might include a table that lists the categories of behaviors that you coded in your study, with the operational definition and inter-rater reliability for each. The format for numbering, title, heading, notes, and rules for such a table remain the same.

Notes. Three different sorts of notes can accompany a table. Each is typed at the bottom of the table in the following sequence:

a. A **general note** provides information that's relevant to the whole table. In our earlier example of Table 3, two general notes were included. The first informed the reader that the maximum score possible in each cell was 20. The second informed the reader of the cell sizes ($\underline{n}$ = 22). As illustrated in that example, you refer to a general note by writing Note (underlined) followed by a period. Then present your information.

b. **A specific note** refers to one particular entry or column. Indicate a specific note using superscripts in lowercase letters ([a], [b], etc.). In Table 3, there were two specific notes. One explained the way in which the Age variable was calculated. The second provided information relevant to the scores of one group of subjects.

c. **Probability levels** indicate the results from your tests of statistical significance. Use one asterisk to indicate the lowest level of significance to which you're referring, then add another asterisk for each higher level included:

$\underline{r}$
.13
.74**
.25*

*$\underline{p}$ < .05. **$\underline{p}$ < .01.

The Use of Figures. Like tables, figures are numbered consecutively, in the order in which they are mentioned in your text. Figures may include photographs, line drawings, graphs, or charts. They can be particularly useful for illustrating complex stimuli, or for presenting patterns of data (e.g., changes across time, or interactions between variables). If your figure is plotting data, it should always present the independent variable on the horizontal axis and the dependent variable on the vertical axis. Clearly label each axis (typing labels parallel to the axis), and indicate the unit of measure for each. Line graphs should only be used to represent continuous data (e.g., time, age, IQ). Use a bar graph to represent discontinuous data (e.g., gender, intervention group). Don't use colors to indicate different functions. Instead, use continuous and discontinuous lines, or geometric symbols for each separate function. In con-

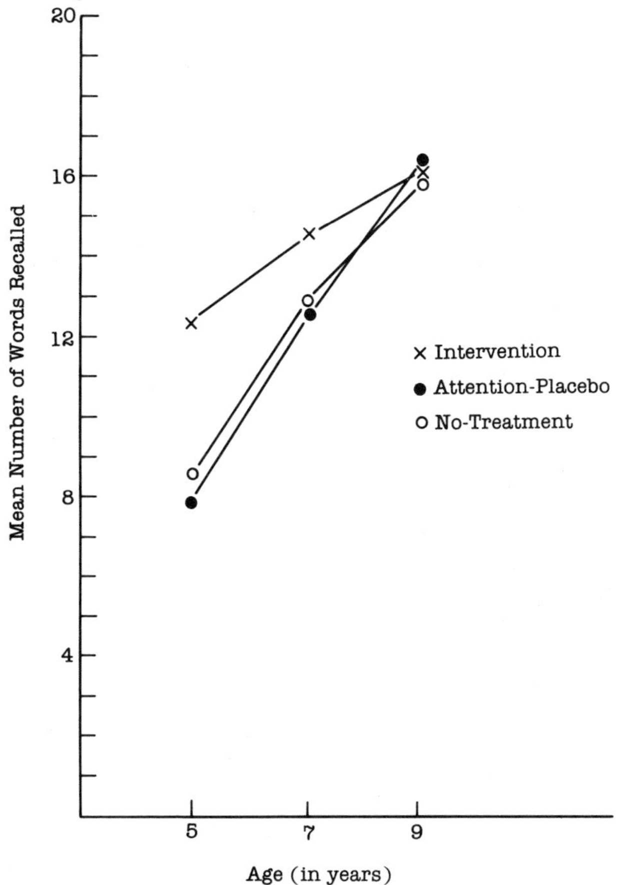

Figure 1 Mean number of words recalled as a function of age

trast to tables, the figure caption is typed *below* the figure. If you are submitting your paper for publication, the caption should be typed on a separate page titled "Figure Captions" (see APA, 1983, p. 147 for further details on publication format).

Figure 1 depicts the information that was presented in Table 3. Figures are often less precise than tables in revealing exact data points, but they can present a better overview of the information.

Your decision about which to use will depend upon the nature of your data and the statement you wish to emphasize.

Using tables and figures from other sources. If you use a table from another source, use a general note to cite the original author(s) in the following manner:

```
Note. From "Information processing rates in the el-
derly" by J. Cerella, 1985, Psychological Bulletin,
98, p. 77.
```

If you are using a figure from another source, include the citation at the end of the figure caption, instead. When planning to submit your report for publication, you need to indicate who holds the copyright for the article, and state that you have obtained permission to reproduce or adapt all or part of the table or figure.

Placement of tables and figures. APA (1983) publication format requires that you type each table and each figure on a separate page, and include them at the end of your paper. Arrange first the tables, and then the figures, in numerical order. The following excerpt from a paper illustrates how you indicate the placement of the table (or figure) in your text:

```
Table 2 presents the cell means. As can be seen,

                ________________________
                 Insert Table 2 about here
                ________________________

the youngest individuals in the intervention group
scored considerably . . . .
```

When preparing a paper for a course or degree requirement, your instructor might prefer that you include your tables and figures in the text rather than use publication format. Check with your instructor before typing your final draft.

WRITING 7.2: YOUR RESULTS. Write a draft of your Results section. Take care to follow the guidelines described above. Address your results according to the sequence in which you made your predictions. Introduce each finding with a brief statement summarizing the result, then present your data and analyses to justify your statement. Be clear and efficient. Consider the advantages and disadvantages of using tables and/or figures to present findings. If appropriate, use one (or both) to supplement your text. As you draft your Results, use your journal to record thoughts and questions concerning modifications or additions to other sections of your report.

Discussion

It's common to feel a bit lost when you come to writing the Discussion section of your report. Your task is to **evaluate** and **interpret** the results of your experiment, rather than simply summarize them. You may feel that you've got nothing to say; the conclusions may seem obvious. Or perhaps the prospect of evaluating and interpreting is overwhelming. Try the following guidelines to structure your discussion; they should make your task more manageable. And, if you've been keeping a lab journal along the way, you'll have a good start on dealing with these issues.

1. Begin your discussion with a clear statement of whether or not your findings confirmed your hypothesis.

2. Relate your findings to the issues you raised in the report introduction. Explain how your research contributes to a further understanding of the experimental problem. If your results confirmed your hypothesis, this task may be relatively straightforward. If they did not confirm your hypothesis, or provided only partial support, your job might be more complex. In any case, note the similarities between your work and the work of others (which you should have outlined in your introduction). This comparison will help you and your reader to understand your findings.

3. Try to interpret your unexpected findings. For example, you could discuss them in terms of reformulated hypotheses that may be based on previous or additional reading. If you find yourself introducing new background literature in your discussion, consider whether that material should be integrated into your introduction. If, after careful thought, you find that you're unable to interpret your results, just say so. Avoid long rationalizations; keep your speculation concise and closely related to empirical data or theory.

You can comment upon the shortcomings of your study, but be concise and avoid apologies (e.g., I should have. . . . If I had. . . . etc.).

4. State the major conclusions from your study. Take care not to over- or understate your points.

5. Present theoretical and practical implications of your study (e.g., suggested modifications of a theoretical stance, implications of your findings for education, counseling, medical practice, etc.).

6. State the implications of your study for future research. Be specific. The cliché, "future research is needed to clarify these issues," is translated by the reader to mean, "I can't think of what to say or where to go from here." If you don't really have anything else to say, then end your discussion there. Don't give lip service to vague and nebulous possibilities.

As you draft your Discussion, you may find gaps or inconsistencies in earlier sections of your report. For example, you may have failed to mention a characteristic of your design which could have affected your results (for example, one group of subjects completed their assessments during the evening, when they may have been tired). Don't feel constrained by what you've written in earlier sections; stay open to new insights and modify the rest of your paper accordingly.

The Discussion section immediately follows your Results (do not begin a new page). The heading "Discussion" (in uppercase and lowercase letters) is centered on the first line. The following is the Discussion section from "Effects of Social Skills Training on Play of Second-Graders," the student paper we began to examine in Chapter 6. Notice how well it follows the guidelines just described.

Discussion

This study failed to confirm the hypothesis that the SST group would show greater improvement in socially competent behavior than the attention-placebo control. Over the eight-week intervention, the SST subjects did not experience greater gains in prosocial behavior nor did they show greater decreases in antisocial behavior. This contrasts with findings in the previous literature. However, those studies typically have used no-treatment controls as their comparison group, and have measured treatment effects with peer- and teacher-report measures rather than behavioral observations.

In fact, across groups, there were some increases in prosocial behavior and decreases in antisocial/aggressive behavior. Thus, to a limited degree, both groups seemed to have benefited from their "treatment" experiences. Although the attention-placebo group was not aimed at increasing social skills, this may have inadvertently occurred since, by design, it was an interaction-oriented group, involving collaborative efforts and group cohesiveness. In retrospect, it seems that these qualities within the group may have enhanced prosocial behaviors and discouraged aggressive, dominant behaviors. Those few studies which used attention-placebo groups in the past did not conduct behavioral observations of subjects (Salton, 1985; Zeyber, 1984). Peer and teacher reports may not be sensitive to the subtle behavioral changes that the attention-placebo experience produces. In fact, even the procedures for behavioral observation in the present study may have limited the demonstrated effectiveness of the interventions. Two 10-minute observational periods per child may not have been long enough to obtain representative samples of play behaviors.

In several instances, intervention effects did not appear until follow-up assessments. This suggests that the beneficial effects of both programs continues to build after the formal meetings have ended. Therefore, future research should pay closer attention to delayed effects, and might profit from using longer follow-up periods.

In conclusion, it appears that social skills interventions can lead to increased prosocial behaviors and decreased antisocial behaviors among second-graders. However, it is not clear that the specific components of SST programs are superior to simple collaborative interaction (i.e., the activities of the attention-placebo). Future research in this area should use longer behavioral observation periods and longer periods before follow-up assessments. The relationship between behavioral observation data and peer and teacher reports should also be examined.

WRITING 7.3: YOUR DISCUSSION. Write a draft of your discussion, using the procedures we've described. Be certain to incorporate the issues you've raised in your lab journal. At the same time, use your journal to note questions and topics which need to be considered in revising earlier sections of your report. Does your discussion flow logically from your introduction? Given your method and results, are your conclusions justified?

References

List full APA documentation of every source you cited in your report. Chapter 9 details the format and procedure for assembling your reference section. Although you should have included a complete reference list in your research proposal, it's likely that you added and deleted some citations as you developed your report. Assemble your reference list once you've completed — but not typed — the final draft of your paper. Then compare them with your text to check for inconsistencies in names and dates. As in the research proposal, your reference section should begin on a new page with the heading "References" (in uppercase and lowercase letters) centered on the first line. Number the reference pages consecutively with the rest of the text and include the short title in the top right corner.

Appendixes

It's rare to include appendixes in publications, but you may find them useful for or even required by some research reports. Appendixes should be used only for supplementary information, that is, information which is useful but not essential for understanding, evaluating, or replicating your experiment. Examples include instructions for debriefing subjects, the subject consent form, or a copy of one of your instruments. Appendixes are labeled with uppercase letters (A, B, C, etc.) in the order in which they are referred to in your report. Refer to each appendix at a relevant point in your text. For example:

> A modified version of Lawson, et al.'s (1979) social self-esteem inventory (see Appendix B) was administered following the exam.

Author Notes

It's unlikely that you'll need to include author notes in a paper for a course assignment. They are included in reports submitted for publication to acknowledge financial or personal assistance in conducting the study, to comment on a change in the author's institutional affiliation, and to note the author's mailing address for reprints or other communication. Author notes begin a new page with the heading "Author Notes" centered at the top. Here is an example:

```
                                  Effects of Social
                                                 12

                      Author Notes

     This study was part of a larger doctoral dis-
sertation project conducted by Stephanie Creedon,
Department of Psychology, University of Vermont.
     The author gratefully acknowledges the assis-
tance of Stephanie Creedon in the design and execu-
tion of the study, and David Howell and Larry Gor-
don in the statistical analyses.
     Additional information regarding the content
of the training programs can be obtained from the
author at the Department of Psychology, University
of Vermont, Burlington, VT, 05405.
```

Footnotes

The use of footnotes is discouraged, since they can be distracting to the reader; their information should be incorporated into the text instead. However, if you must include footnotes, they should be indicated by a superscript arabic numeral in the text, numbered in sequence throughout your paper. Type the footnote information on a new page, headed "Footnotes," and insert it following Author Notes. Here is an example:

```
                                  Effects of Social

                                                 13

                       Footnotes

     [1]Complete descriptions of the training proce-
dures and the stimuli are available from the
author.
     [2]These analyses were also conducted by enter-
ing each group of variables together and then using
the best predictor from each group when all other
groups were considered. Identical results emerged.
```

Tables, Figure Captions, and Figures

If you're using APA (1983) publication format, your tables should be assembled, in consecutive order, following your reference list. Your Figure Caption page should follow, listing each figure caption in sequence. Here's an example:

Perspective-taking

17

Figure Captions

Figure 1. Schematic view of the perspective-taking apparatus.

Figure 2. Mean proportion of problems solved as a function of IQ and training experience.

Then include your figures in consecutive order as well. Be certain to check with your instructor on whether you should include the tables and figures within your text instead.

REVISING YOUR REPORT

As we've mentioned elsewhere in this text, revision is an essential part of any writing. It is certainly true when drafting a research report. You may have conscientiously worked on each section of your paper, but until you read it as a whole, you can't judge the degree to which it conveys a clear, coherent message and represents a logical integration of material. As you read your report from start to finish, you'll probably discover that information is missing, incomplete, or inconsistent among the sections. As we suggested in revising your research proposal, (a) begin by considering the whole proposal, checking for continuity and coherence; (b) then focus on whether each individual section is accurate and complete; (c) finally, focus on the details of style: word choice, punctuation, and other elements of grammar that add clarity and precision to individual paragraphs and sentences (see Chapters 10 and 11 for assistance).

Get away from your report for a while before you complete your revisions — this will help you take a fresh look at it, as your reader will ultimately do. And ask a couple of classmates or friends to read it over. This peer review is so helpful that many instructors require it as part of the assignment. Remember that the kind of feedback someone can provide will depend upon the state of your paper. If the draft is rough, the feedback can be more general; if the draft is more refined, the feedback can be more specific. Therefore, *before* you ask someone to review your draft, complete the revising procedure we've described above — for their sake and yours!

> WRITING 7.4: REVISING. Get away from your paper for at least a few hours, preferably for a few days. Then revise using the guidelines we've described. Have a couple of classmates read your report, and incorporate their feedback in your revisions. After you've typed your paper, *proofread* it carefully. Then make a photocopy of it, just in case you or your instructor misplaces or loses the original.

CHECKLIST FOR THE RESEARCH REPORT

The APA (1983, p. 29) publication manual suggests a number of questions which may help you assess the quality of your report. Drawing upon these, as well as the information we've presented in this chapter, we suggest you ask yourself the following:

1. Title Page (page 1)

Is your title informative and accurate? Does it indicate your independent and dependent variables?

Does your title page follow the format shown on page 113, or requested by your instructor or editor?

2. Abstract (page 2)

Is the abstract 150 words or less?

Does your abstract comprehensively summarize the problem, subjects, procedures, results, and conclusions of your study?

3. Introduction (begins on page 3 with title of paper on the first line)

Does your introduction clearly describe: (a) the problem, (b) the relevant background literature, (c) the rationale for your specific experimental design, and (d) your formal hypothesis (or hypotheses)?

4. Method (immediately follows Introduction)

Is your description clear enough to allow others to replicate your study?

Have you described your subjects, apparatus, instruments, materials, and procedures in adequate detail?

Have you specified your method of data analysis (if one was used)?

5. Results (immediately follows Method)

Are the results organized according to your predictions?

Have you clearly described your summary data and the results of your statistical analyses?

Are your tables and figures in proper format and numerical sequence?

Does the narrative explain the significance of each table and figure?

6. Discussion (immediately follows Results)

Do you interpret and evaluate your results in terms of the issues raised in your introduction?

Does your discussion remain focused upon issues that are directly relevant to your study?

Do you state your conclusions and address the implications or applications of your findings?

7. References (begins a new page)

Have you listed every reference you cited in your report, and only those sources?

Are your references in full APA documentation style and arranged in alphabetical order?

Have you actually read all the references you list?

Overall Considerations

Have you included all appropriate citations?

Have you used APA format (or the format requested by your instructor or editor) for ordering and presenting information *throughout* your report?

Does your paper present its findings in a logical manner — from paragraph to paragraph, as well as section to section?

HAVE YOU PROOFREAD YOUR FINAL DRAFT?

Have you photocopied your paper?

[8] *Principles of Library Research and Basic Bibliographies*

PREVIEW:

If you are asked to write a research paper or report — even if it's brief — you'll need to spend some time becoming acquainted with your college library. This can be intimidating since most libraries house an impressive amount of information. How can you move through the library's sea of resources and get to the relevant material?

THE PRELIMINARIES

This chapter will show you how to identify and locate relevant materials in psychology and take notes from them for your paper. Here are four points to keep in mind before you actually begin working in the library:

1. There's too much to see in Rome in a day. You don't need to understand the entire library system — just focus on that part which will help you find the books and articles you need.

2. Reference librarians do not bite. In fact, our own experience in many libraries would have been frustrating and aimless without the experienced help of reference librarians. Remember, these people have made a profession out of knowing where information is stored and how to retrieve it. Like all good professionals, they want to share their expertise. Talk to them. They're usually in the reference section itself.

3. You can't tell the players without a program. Somewhere on the ground floor of your library are information packets containing floor plans of the library. If you study one of these maps carefully you can usually locate the general areas of the library that contain literature in your field. Also, most libraries have free tours offered at a variety of convenient times. Try one.

4. Read the back pages. Check references cited in your textbook; they may be listed at the end of individual chapters or at the end of the book. There you should find a list of additional reading ranging from journal articles and book chapters to entire books. Since textbooks typically cite the "classics" in the field, they are a good place to start (and subsequently develop) your literature search — one or two comprehensive bibliographical references can open up an entire field.

TAKING NOTES

Purchase a supply of 3″ × 5″ and 4″ × 6″ lined index cards to use for recording references and taking notes from the literature:

1. Reference cards. Use the 3″ × 5″ cards for recording the references you find. Write them in full APA format (described in Chapter 9). If you get used to using APA format whenever you're noting a reference, it will become second nature to you. On the top line, record the author's (or authors') last name, first and middle initials, and the date of publication in parentheses. On the second line record the title of the book or article. For a book, include the city of publication and the name of the publisher on subsequent lines. For a journal, enter the name of the journal, its volume number, and inclusive pages (see Chapter 9 for APA format). When dealing with books, use the bottom of the reference card for recording the library call number once you find it. Figure 8.1 on page 166 shows examples of reference cards for a chapter in a book and for a journal article.

The advantage of constructing reference cards in this way is that once you've completed your paper, your reference list can be compiled simply by alphabetizing the cards which correspond to the citations in your paper.

2. Topic cards. As you assemble a list of sources relevant to your research, you should begin reading and reviewing several of these references; this can help direct and refine your search for other material. Use 4″ × 6″ cards for taking notes from your references. Because you have complete bibliographic information recorded on the reference cards, you needn't repeat it on each topic card. Rather, your topic cards should include the following:

a. Place a heading on the top line which describes the subject of the specific material you're noting. These headings might ultimately make up the topics and subtopics of your paper's outline. For example, let's say that you're writing a paper on childhood psychosis. Each time you come across an article that defines "psychosis" in a unique way, you might note the definition and label the card "definition of psychosis."
b. Record the material from your source that's relevant to your paper. First read the article quickly without writing a thing, in order to get a sense of its complete message. Then read it more slowly and carefully, taking notes on the most important issues. Write no more than *one* central idea on each card. Then you'll be able to reorganize your cards by subtopics rather than by source when it's time to outline and

Reference card for chapter in a book

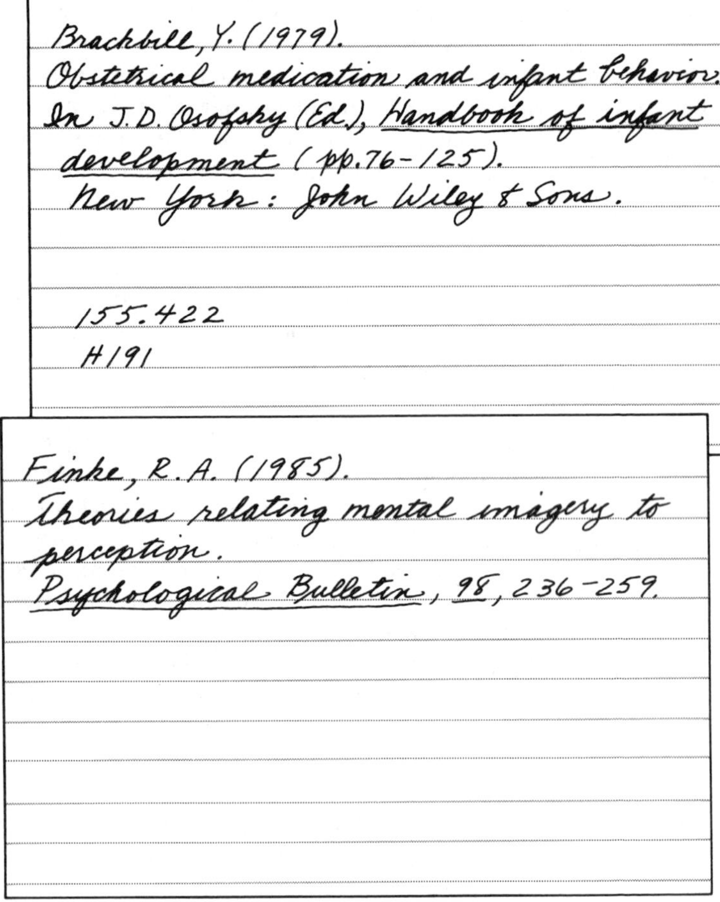
Brackbill, Y. (1979).
Obstetrical medication and infant behavior.
In J.D. Osofsky (Ed.), Handbook of infant
development (pp. 76-125).
New York: John Wiley & Sons.

155.422
H191

Finke, R.A. (1985).
Theories relating mental imagery to
perception.
Psychological Bulletin, 98, 236-259.

Reference card for journal article

Figure 8.1 *Sample reference cards*

draft your paper. Summarize the information in your own words whenever possible. Use quotations only when the author has a unique or compelling statement you want to capture. Remember that these notes represent the foundations of your research; from them you will build and advance an argument of your own. Therefore, be certain that your summary and analysis are accurate. Whenever you use the words, ideas, data, or reasonings of another writer, you're responsible for representing that author's work fairly and precisely. Chapters 3 and 4 discuss how to analyze and summarize the literature. Review those sections before you begin these tasks.

c. Include a citation (rather than a full reference) of your source using APA format (author name and date).
d. Note your reactions to the information you've recorded (does it raise questions; is it based on firm logic, etc.). On the other hand, you might find it helpful to record some of these sorts of reactions on separate topic cards so that you can reassemble them independently of the original source when preparing to draft your paper.

Figure 8.2 on p. 168 is an example of a topic note card written while preparing a paper on friendship patterns among retarded individuals.

WRITING 8.1: PREPARING TO USE THE LIBRARY. List two possible paper topics for your psychology course. Compile a list of preliminary sources for your topic using your textbook and other books in your room. Record these preliminary references on note cards, as described above.

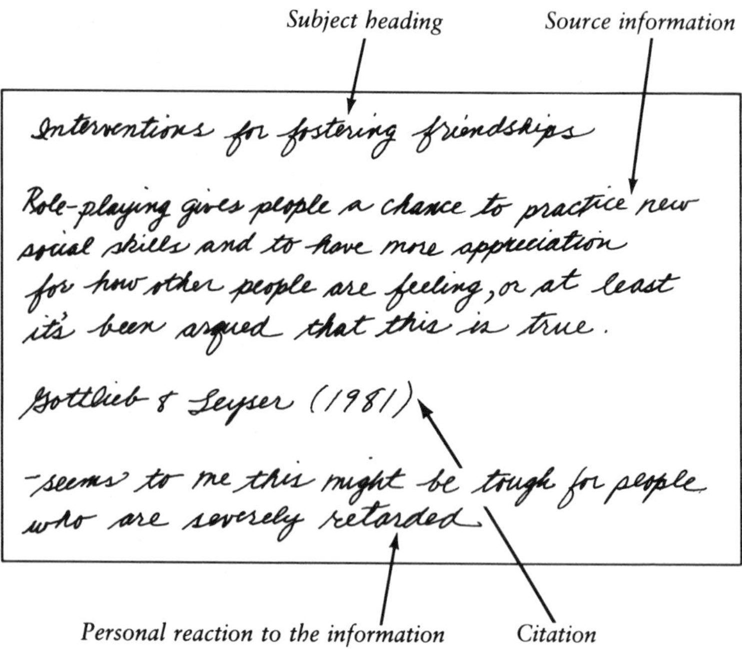

Figure 8.2 *Sample note card*

FINDING BOOKS

Most students were introduced to library card catalogs long before going to college. To obtain a book, look it up in the card catalog using its title or author's name. When you find the book card, its call numbers tell you where it is located on the library shelves. Along with the call numbers, the card includes the complete names of both book and author(s) as well as other information about the book itself. Figure 8.3 shows examples of book cards.

If your library has "closed stacks," access to the book shelves is restricted, and you'll need to fill out and submit a **call slip** — a card identifying what you need.

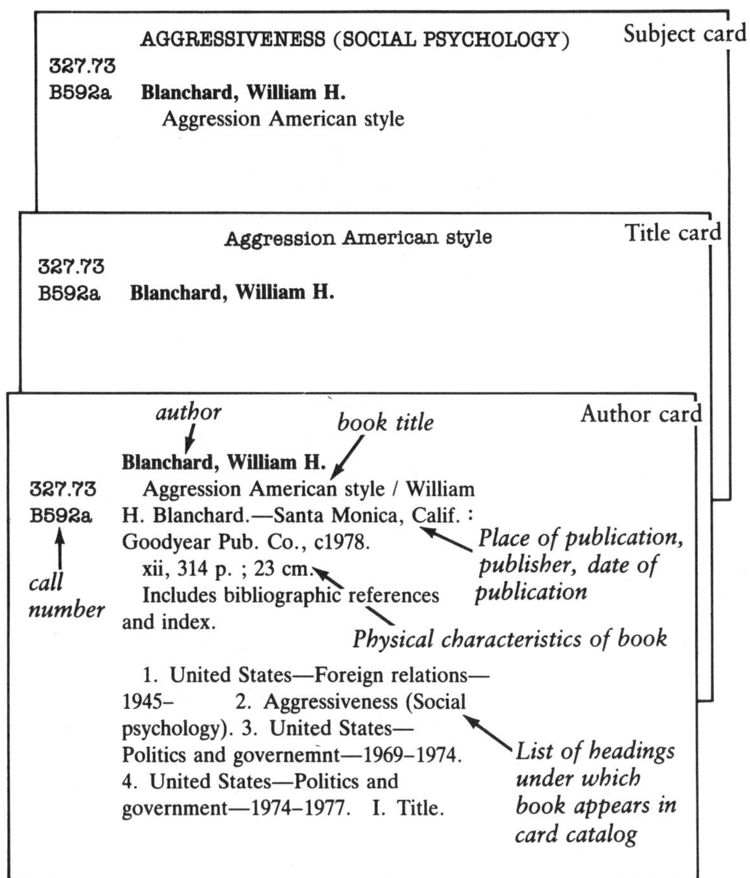

Figure 8.3 *William H. Blanchard's* Aggression American Style *as it appears in the card catalog*

WRITING 8.2: USING THE CARD CATALOG'S AUTHOR OR TITLE INDEX. Find the call numbers for each of the books you included in your preliminary list of references (Writing 8.1). Record the call numbers on the corresponding reference cards.

The procedure just described is simple enough when you know which book you want. But what if you are just beginning your research and would like to discover what books are available on your topic? Turn to the **Subject Index** of your library's card catalog system (see the example of a Subject Card in Figure 8.3). The Subject Index organizes references by topic. How do you know which specific subject heading to use? One of the most widely used listings of subjects is the *Library of Congress Subject Headings.* If you were interested in obtaining information on books about child psychopathology, for example, Figure 8.4 shows the topics you would find relevant to your subject from the *Library of Congress Subject Headings.*

The entry, **Child psychopathology,** appears in boldface, indicating that it's a main heading. Underneath this topic are several subdivisions and cross-references. The *sa* means *see also,* and there follows a list of eight more specific terms that you could use, instead of **Child psychopathology,** to narrow down your search. For example, the listing indicates that if you wish to focus specifically on **Schizophrenia in children,** the *Library of Congress Subject Headings* provides headings from within that specialization. Further down the list you'll note an *x,* identifying a *see from* reference. This indicates that the terms *Children — Mental Disorders, Mental illness in children,* and *Psychopathology, Child,* are not used as subject headings; if you attempt to look up any of these titles, they will refer you to the main heading, *Child psychopathology.* The *xx* subdivision which follows means *see also from.* The entries under this category — for example, *Child mental health* and *Child psychiatry* — are broader than the topic *Child psychopathology;* therefore, refer to this list only if you want to enlarge your reference scope.

WRITING 8.3: USING THE CARD CATALOG'S SUBJECT INDEX. Go to the *Library of Congress Subject Headings* and find the main heading for your proposed writing topic. Use two or more of the subject headings you find, consult your library's card catalog, and create reference cards for what appear to be important books on your topic.

sa Psychological tests for children
— Vocational guidance (*Indirect*)
x Child psychology as a profession
xx Psychologists
Child psychology as a profession
See Child psychology — Vocational guidance
Child psychopathology (*RJ499*)
Here are entered descriptive works on mental disorders of children. Works on the clinical and therapeutic aspects of mental disorders in children are entered under Child psychiatry. Works on mentally ill children themselves are entered under Mentally ill children.
sa Autism
Child psychiatry
Depression in children
Emotional problems of children
Mentally handicapped children
Mentally ill children
Psychoses in children
Schizophrenia in children
x Children — Mental disorders
Mental illness in children
Psychopathology, Child
xx Child mental health
Child psychiatry
Emotional problems of children
Psychology, Pathological
Notes under Child psychiatry; Mentally ill children
Child psychotherapy (*Indirect*)
sa Child analysis
Play therapy
xx Child mental health services

Figure 8.4 *Entries for Child psychopathology in the* Library of Congress Subject Headings *(1980, p. 399)*

FINDING PERIODICALS

The process of publishing a book is time consuming. Several years typically elapse between the time the author completes a draft and the arrival of the book at your library. Thus, a book is not always representative of the most recent knowledge in the field. While journal material often is not as elaborate as that in books, it has the advantage of being current and concise. However, students writing research reports often underestimate the importance of professional journals or are unaware of how to use them.

Most libraries house their periodicals in a separate section. The periodical titles are arranged alphabetically on open shelves. In other libraries journals are kept in a restricted area, but it is possible to obtain an article by presenting its reference information to the periodical desk librarian. Most libraries maintain a list of the periodicals that they hold so that you don't have to wade through the aisles to see if they stock a particular journal. Also, if your library doesn't have a certain journal, it's often possible to obtain the article you need through the interlibrary loan system. Ask the reference librarian about this.

There are literally hundreds of journals that deal with issues relevant to psychology. Material on any given topic can be found in a variety of them. For example, infant development is discussed in *Child: Care, Health and Development, Child Care Quarterly, Child Development, Child Study Journal, Developmental Psychology, Developmental Review, First Language, Human Development, Infant Behavior and Development, Infant Mental Health Journal, Journal of Experimental Child Psychology, Journal of Genetic Psychology, Journal of Obstetric, Gynecologic, and Neonatal Nursing, Journal of Pediatric Psychology, Merrill-Palmer Quarterly, Monographs of the Society for Research in Child Development,* and other journals. Therefore, it would be incredibly inefficient to research a topic by simply thumbing through one journal issue after another. Two types of systems have been developed to help researchers find information in periodicals. One uses indexes; the other uses abstracts (the standardized summary described in Chapter 4).

Using *Psychological Abstracts*

Psychological Abstracts (commonly referred to as *Psych Abstracts*) is the most comprehensive listing of articles published in the field of psychology. Each month, indexers from *Psych Abstracts* scan many journals from psychology and its related fields, such as sociology, education, psychiatry, medicine, biology, and social work.

They assemble abstracts of the most recently published literature, and categorize and index these abstracts by topic. So, using *Psych Abstracts,* you can identify all the research on a given topic without having to skim the journals. All you need to do is establish the general subject area you wish to research. At the back of each volume of *Psych Abstracts* is an index of subject headings which identifies, by number, the abstracts that are relevant to your topic. Jot down the numbers, and look up each in that year's volume (due to its size, one volume may be bound in several books). For each article, you'll find complete bibliographic information and an abstract. If the abstract suggests that the information will be useful for your research, go to the original source. Generally, that's all there is to it.

Here is the procedure for using *Psychological Abstracts:*

Step 1: The Thesaurus of Psychological Index Terms

The *Thesaurus* is located in the reference section of your library. This book lists, alphabetically, the exact terms which are used in the *Psych Abstracts'* subject indexes. Rather than guessing which subject heading is appropriate for your topic, you can identify it here.

Suppose you were interested in reference material on childhood psychosis. The term is listed in bold print in the *Thesaurus* (see Figure 8.5, pg. 174), indicating that it is indeed a topic that can be found among *Psych Abstracts* subject headings. The abbreviations and terms directly underneath the boldface entry provide further information on the topic heading (the notations are explained in the front pages of the *Thesaurus*).

Step 2: The Brief Subject Index

At the back of each monthly issue of *Psych Abstracts* is the Brief Subject Index. When the monthly issues are bound by year, two Volume Indexes are created (each indexing six of the issues of *Psych Abstracts* published that year). Locate your subject heading in the index and it will list a series of numbers after it, each of which refers to an abstract of an article on your topic.

Childhood Psychosis[67]
PN 399 SC 08790
UF Infantile Psychosis
B Psychosis[67]
N Childhood Schizophrenia[67]
Early Infantile Autism[73]
Symbiotic Infantile Psychosis[73]
R Autistic Children[73]
Emotionally Disturbed[73]

Childhood Schizophrenia[67]
PN 494 SC 08800
B Childhood Psychosis[67]
Psychosis[67]
Schizophrenia[67]
R Early Infantile Autism[73]
Symbiotic Infantile Psychosis[73]

Childlessness[82]
PN 36 SC 08805
SN State of having no children.
B Family Structure[73]
Parenthood Status[86]
R Delayed Parenthood[86]
Family Planning Attitudes[73]

Childrearing Attitudes[73]
PN 432 SC 08810
R Attitudes/[87]
Family Relations[87]
Parental Attitudes[73]

Figure 8.5 Thesaurus of Psychological Index Terms *(4th ed., 1985, p. 34)*

Childhood Play Development 25605, 27631, 28357, 28392, 31078, 31131
Childhood Psychosis [See Also Childhood Schizophrenia, Early Infantile Autism] 27281, 29273, 30010, 31442, 31489
Childhood Schizophrenia 25952, 28822
Childlessness 28358
Childrearing Attitudes 25589, 25734, 31105, 31196, 31217, 31416, 32744

Figure 8.6 Psychological Abstracts *(Vol. 71, December 1984, p. viii)*

For example, Figure 8.6, an excerpt from Volume 71, December 1984, of *Psych Abstracts* lists the term *Childhood Psychosis* with five entry numbers. This means that there are five references abstracted in the current volume which deal specifically with childhood psychosis.

Step 3: The Abstracts

Look up each abstract that is listed under your topic. Remember that the entry numbers are abstract numbers, not page numbers; the abstracts are ordered sequentially in the text of *Psych Abstracts*. For example, the second entry number listed under the heading **Childhood Psychosis** was 29273. If you located this abstract, you'd find the entry shown in Figure 8.7.

The entry number 29273 is followed by the author's name, Deborah L. Browning, and in parentheses, her institutional affiliation at the time the article was written (Yale School of Medicine). The title of Browning's article appears next, **Control and Transitional Reality in the Treatment of a Psychotic Child,** followed by the name and date of the journal in which it was published, ***Bulletin of Menninger Clinic,*** **March 1984, Volume 48, issue number 2,**

29273. **Browning, Deborah L.** (Yale U School of Medicine, Yale Psychiatric Inst) **Control and transitional reality in the treatment of a psychotic child.** *Bulletin of the Menninger Clinic,* 1984(Mar), Vol 48(2), 141–154. — Describes the difficulties involved in communicating with a severely disturbed 8-year-old child on her terms — through her motorically enacted fantasies — and in bringing her forward, once a relationship was established, into a more realistic, representational world. The therapist used titrated doses of nonmetaphoric interventions, straight talk, and limit-setting to gently push the psychotic S through the more delusional aspects of therapy. Their playing out of S's fantasies were initially characterized by S's efforts at control, high activity level, and insistence that the fantasies were actually reality. The author contends that S had to control the objects in her world if they were to be tools to help her with the tasks of mastery; at the same time, S had to learn to master a world over which she had less and less illusory control. Such a difficult task becomes even more difficult with older or more disturbed children. (10 ref) — *Journal abstract.*

Figure 8.7 Psychological Abstracts *(Vol. 71, December 1984, p. 3117)*

pages 141–154. This bibliographic information allows you to get the journal article yourself if you decide you want to. The abstract comes next, followed by the notation "(10 ref)". This means that Browning's article includes references to ten other sources, a fact which may prove useful as you try to gather more research on your topic. Once you read the abstract, you can decide whether this article might be worth reading in full for your research.

> WRITING 8.4: USING *PSYCH ABSTRACTS.* Use the *Thesaurus of Psychological Index of Terms* to find and list at least three subject headings relevant to your research topic. Refer to a recent issue of *Psych Abstracts* and use the headings to find two articles relevant to your topic. Check to see that the articles are in journals your library owns. If not, find two new ones. Then record each reference on a 3″ × 5″ reference card, using standard APA format (Chapter 9).

Author Indexes to Psych Abstracts

At times you might be aware that a particular author has published an article on your topic, but you don't know exactly where or when the article was published. In this case, the *Author Index to Psychological Abstracts* can be helpful. Simply look up the author's last name in the *Author Index* and you'll find the same entry number which was presented in the Brief Subject Index. Use the *Author Index* that corresponds to the year in which the article was published, or the following year (there is a slight delay between the time the article is published and the time it is included in *Psych Abstracts*). For example, had you known that in 1984 Deborah Browning published a report on childhood psychosis, you could have looked up Browning's last name in the 1984 volume of the *Author Index* and found the entry shown in Figure 8.8.

Cumulated Indexes to Psych Abstracts

Every two years a cumulated catalog of subject and author indexes is published by the APA. They cover several volumes of *Psych Abstracts,* listing the subjects in one edition and the authors in another. As illustrated in Figure 8.9, an excerpt from the *Cumulated Subject Index* for 1978–80, you'll find brief descriptions of re-

Browning, Chris — *See* Lenney, Ellen 15002, 28651
Browning, Deborah L. Aspects of authoritarian attitudes in ego development. *Journal of Personality & Social Psychology, 1983(Jul), Vol 45(1), 137–144.* 6417
Browning, Deborah L. Control and transitional reality in the treatment of a psychotic child. *Bulletin of the Menninger Clinic, 1984(Mar), Vol 48(2), 141–154.* 29273
Browning, Ellen R. A memory pacer for improving stimulus generalization. *Journal of Autism & Developmental Disorders, 1983(Dec), Vol 13(4), 427–432.* 11059

Figure 8.8 *Entries for Deborah L. Browning from the* Author Index to Psychological Abstracts *(Vol. 71, December 1984, p. 143)*

Childhood Psychosis [See Also Childhood Schizophrenia. Early Infantile Autism. Symbiotic Infantile Psychosis]
affect & cognition, Piagetian one-to-one correspondence & class inclusion tasks performance, psychotic children, implications for convergence theory of development, 59:10028
amino compounds & organic acids in cerebrospinal fluid & plasma & urine, psychotic children, 63:7714
bipolar distribution of childhood psychosis, 3–5 yr olds, 63:1091
brain damage, subsequent autistic symptoms & postencephalitic psychosis, previously normal 10 yr old male, 64:12604
characteristics of schematic models of eyes out of context with human face, gaze aversion, normal vs psychotic 3–14 yr olds, 64:12617
child guidance clinic with multidisciplinary treatment approach, 2–6 yr old patients with mostly Down's syndrome & psychosis, 64:10972
childhood psychosis, historical aspects & diagnosis, 62:8779
child's severe & chronically disabling cognitive & behavioral disorder, family adaptation & patterns of coping & social relations, parents of psychotic children, 60:3214
clinical manifestations, infantile psychoses, 6–10 yr olds, 61:3792
cognitive functioning, psychotic children, 62:6121
co-occurrence of mental retardation & endogenous & reactive & episodic psychosis, children, 61:3707
death & psychosis & obsession, analysis of familial antecedents of psychotic vs normal children, 60:11877
development & administration & scoring of Children's Handicaps & Behavior & Skills interview schedule, severely mentally retarded & psychotic children, 61:12382
development of pronoun usage in statements expressing concepts of possession & action & description, psychotic 5–16 yr olds, 62:6221
dopamine & serotonin metabolism, neuropsychiatrically disturbed children, 59:5771
early maternal separation, borderline personality vs psychotic vs other psychiatric disorders, children & adolescents, 62:6128
evolution of nosography of childhood psychoses, 61:13522
haloperidol, children with behavior disorders & acute anxiety & psychoneurosis & psychosis, 61:4251
intellectual characteristics, psychotic adolescents with high verbal ability, 60:1257

Figure 8.9 *Entries on Childhood Psychosis from the* Cumulated Subject Index to Psychological Abstracts *1978–1980 (p. 381)*

search on childhood psychosis published during this time period, accompanied by the volume and entry numbers identifying where the article is indexed in *Psych Abstracts*.

The cumulated indexes avoid laboring with the individual volume indexes. But be forewarned: Because the cumulated indexes are published every two years, a gap occurs in their coverage of the most recent scholarship. For work printed since the latest issue of the *Cumulated Index*, it's necessary to rely on one or more of the individual volume indexes.

All of the indexes we've discussed in this chapter are really designed to accomplish the same thing: to help you find sources through *Psych Abstracts*. Obviously the index(es) you choose to use in this process will depend on what you wish to know, what you already know, and the importance of current research to your topic. In general, it's best to begin a bibliographic search by starting with the most recent volume of *Psych Abstracts* and then working your way back through time. However, be aware that some research topics were popular for narrowly defined periods of time. Thus, for example, you might find few references relevant to your topic until you go back as far as 1969, and then find a wealth of information available through the 1960's.

WRITING 8.5: USING THE SUBJECT AND/OR AUTHOR CUMULATED INDEXES TO *PSYCH ABSTRACTS*. Use the cumulated indexes to find the two journal article entries you identified in Writing 8.4. Copy the first line of each entry; be sure that you have found the exact articles you located earlier. If you aren't able to locate these references in the cumulated indexes, is it because they were published too recently to be included?

Other Abstracting Services

Depending upon the topic of your research, you may want to use other abstracting services in addition to, or instead of, *Psych Abstracts*. These include *Animal Behavior Abstracts; Biological Abstracts; Child Development Abstracts and Bibliography; Criminal Justice Abstracts; ERIC, Resources in Education; Psychopharmacology Abstracts;* and *Sociological Abstracts*. Several of these are more narrowly defined than *Psych Abstracts* and are therefore less overwhelming. On the other hand, those that are more narrowly focused are also less comprehensive.

USING CITATION INDEXES

Scholarship does not exist in a vacuum; published articles build on the established knowledge. Citation indexes take advantage of this fact and allow you to find sources that have *cited* particular references you've identified. Thus, citation indexes differ from the techniques we've already discussed in two important ways. First, rather than being retrospective, that is, searching back through time, they allow us to search *forward* in time, starting with the publication of a key paper. Second, rather than requiring subject headings to direct the search, a citation index organizes sources according to the citations they include. Two citation indexes particularly helpful in psychology are the *Social Science Citation Index* (*SSCI*) and the *Science Citation Index* (*SCI*). Each is published annually.

To illustrate their use, let's say that you've come across an article (or a reference to an article) that's exactly what you're looking for — a paper by Donald Forgays and Janet Read on crucial periods for free-environmental experience in the rat. The article was published in 1962 in the *Journal of Comparative and Physiological Psychology*, Volume 55, pages 816–818. You can find the authors, dates and names of publications that have cited this work in any subsequent year by locating **Forgays,** the first author's name, in the citation index. For example, in the 1984 *Social Science Citation Index* we find the entry shown in Figure 8.10 (p. 180).

Each of Forgays' publications that were cited during the indexed period is listed in boldface type — there are three. Each listing includes the year the work was published, the title of the book or journal, the volume number, and the page on which the article begins. Directly beneath each of these entries is information on the publications that have cited Forgays' work, including the first author, an abbreviation for the journal, the volume number, the first page of the article, and the year in which it was published. You can see that Forgays' 1962 article was cited by two authors, Holson and Jouhanea. Jouhanea's article is in *Journal of Comparative Psy-*

FORGAS JP		VOL	PG	YR
KERBER KW	J PERSONAL	52	177	84
FORGATCH M				
83 UNPUB PROBLEM SOLVIN				
PATTERSO.GR	CHILD DEV	55	1299	84
FORGATCH MS				
79 J PEDIATRIC PSYCHOL 4 129				
PATTERSO.GR	AGGR BEHAV	10	253	84
81 UNPUB FAMILY PROB				
CLINGEMP.WG	FAM RELAT	33	465	84
82 TIME OUT VIDEO TRAIN				
PATTERSO.GR	CHILD DEV	55	1299	84
FORGAYS DG				
52 J COMP PHYSIOL PSYCH 45 322				
HOLSON R	PSYCH LEARN R	18	199	84
JURASKA JM	DEVELOP PSY	17	209	84
ROSENZWE.MR	AM PSYCHOL	39	365	84
62 J COMPARATIVE PHYSIO 55 816				
HOLSON R	PSYCH LEARN R	18	199	84
JOUHANEA.J	J COM PSYCH	98	318	84
79 TEACHING PSYCHOL 6 246				
ROGERS A	TEACH PSYCH R	11	59	84
FORGE A				
66 1965 P ROYAL ANTHR 1 23				
BOWDEN R	MAN	19	445	84
70 ASA MONOGRAPHS 8 269				
HERZFELD M	AM ETHNOL	11	439	84
70 SOCIALIZATION APPROA				

Figure 8.10 *Entries for Donald Forgays from the* Social Science Citation Index *(1984)*

chology, Volume 98; it begins on page 318 and was published in 1984. If you wanted to learn more about what Holson and Jouhanea had to say, you could either look up each article in its respective journal or consult the Source Index of the *Social Science Citation Index,* which provides the complete title of each article. Although the *SSCI* is most often used to find topic information, it can also give you a sense of whether a particular author has greatly influenced the scholarship in the field.

WRITING 8.6: USING CITATION INDEXES. Select one of the references you identified in an earlier writing exercise in this chapter and try to locate two articles which have subsequently cited that article. If your original reference is quite recent, you probably won't find citations listed — it takes some time for the original research to be read and responded to, and for those responses to get published and indexed. Of course, it's also possible that over the years, no one has opted to cite a particular article.

COMPUTER SEARCHES

So far in this chapter we have described a variety of traditional methods for building a research bibliography. The computer revolution provides yet another avenue to the information in the library card catalog, indexes, and abstracts. These search systems vary but, typically, references and abstracts are coded in the computer data base according to key words which describe the article (e.g., the variables investigated and the subjects studied). For example, the *Permuterm Subject Index* lists a broad range of publications based on significant words in article titles.

Computer-assisted searches can cover a vast amount of material in a short period of time. However, they also have some drawbacks. First, they can be expensive, especially if you haven't sufficiently narrowed your topic. If your key words are too general, you'll get pages and pages of printout, with only a handful of relevant references. Second, the network you are using may not catalog all the available reference sources, so you may find a few gaps in the material available. Third, this service is sometimes restricted to faculty and/or graduate students; even if it isn't, it's sometimes difficult to secure time on the computer. Finally, and most importantly, the search is only as good as the key words you use. You must take care to be precise and neither too broad nor too narrow in your choice of terms. Check with your reference librarian to see what sorts of computer-assisted searches are available to you. The best time to use a computer search is *after* you have done a good deal of research using the techniques described earlier in this chapter. Once you have narrowed to a specific topic and have identified key words that unlock the index sources, the computer can be useful as a bibliographic cross-check to the material you have assembled by yourself.

A SELECTED GUIDE TO REFERENCE SOURCES IN PSYCHOLOGY

The following are only a few of the many resources available to the researcher in psychology. Use this list as a guide to the major reference materials:

Guides and Bibliographies (each of these books contains detailed information on how to use reference books in psychology)

Bell, J. E. (1971). *A guide to library research in psychology.* Dubuque, IA: W. C. Brown.

Reed, J. G., & Baxter, P. M. (1983). *Library use: A handbook for psychology.* Washington, DC: American Psychological Association.

Indexes

Contemporary Psychology: A Journal of Reviews. Washington, DC: American Psychological Association, 1956 —. [Reviews new books, about 40–50 per issue.]

Cumulative Author Index to Psychological Abstracts. Washington, DC: American Psychological Association, 1969 —.

Cumulative Subject Index to Psychological Abstracts. Washington, DC: American Psychological Association, 1969 —.

Index Medicus. Washington, DC: American Psychological Associates, 1969 —.

Journal Supplement Abstract Service (JSAS) Catalog of Selected Documents in Psychology. Washington, DC: American Psychological Association, 1971 —. [Quarterly until 1983; since then entitled *Psychological Documents.*]

Psychological Abstracts. Washington, DC: American Psychological Association, 1927 —.

Thesaurus of Psychological Index Terms. Washington, DC: American Psychological Association, 1927 —.

Social Science Citation Index. Philadelphia, PA: Institute for Scientific Information. [Published annually since 1969; an accumulated index is available for 1966–1970.]

Science Citation Index. Philadelphia, PA: Institute for Scientific Information. [Published annually since 1961; an accumulated index is available for 1955–1964.]

Dictionaries of Psychological Terms

Chaplin, J. P. (1968). *The dictionary of psychology*. New York: Dell.

English, H. B., & English, A. C. (1958). *A comprehensive dictionary of psychological and psychoanalytic terms*. New York: Longmans.

Hinsie, L. E., & Campbell, R. J. (1970). *Psychiatric dictionary*. New York: Oxford University Press.

Wolman, B. B. (1973). *Dictionary of behavioral science*. New York: Van Nostrand.

[9] *Documentation: Why, When, and How*

PREVIEW:

Reference Citations in Text

Why Use Reference Citations?

When Should You Use Reference Citations?

How Do You Present Reference Citations?

Footnotes

References

Periodicals

Books

Unpublished Sources

Matching References to Citations

Almost everyone who begins a project of research and writing finds the issue of documentation confusing. Should your reference list contain all the books and articles you consulted or only those references cited? Should you use footnotes or in-text citations? The conventions for documentation vary from one discipline to another, so that what is appropriate for your psychology class may not be appropriate for your English course. In fact, you may discover that there are some inconsistencies in format even within psychology.

Why the big fuss? Why does it matter whether you underline rather than use quotations to indicate a book title in your reference list? Why should you be concerned about whether a reference's publication date precedes or follows the author's name, as long as all the information is included? Here's why: Conventions create a predictability and order, and therefore add clarity. They allow us to know how and where to look for the information we are seeking, and how to interpret the information that is presented. The goal of conventions in documentation is to minimize the very sort of confusion that students who are new to a field often experience.

The standard format for documentation in psychology is referred to as APA format because it is established in the *Publication Manual of the American Psychological Association* (1983). Unless you are told otherwise, you should use APA format whenever you write anything for a psychology course. If you are writing for publication, you'll find that APA format is, again, typically what is required. However, be certain to check the journal for which you are writing. Editors spell out their journal's manuscript requirements and other guidelines for contributors generally in the front or the back of the journal.

In the following pages you'll find explanations and examples of the most common types of citations and references. Yet no brief treatment will likely answer all of your questions about manuscript preparation and documentation. If you don't find an answer to your question here, consult with your professor or with the APA manual, which is probably in your library's reference section. If you wish, you can order an APA manual by writing the Order Department, American Psychological Association, 1200 Seventeenth Street, N.W., Washington, D.C. 20036.

REFERENCE CITATIONS IN THE TEXT

Why Use Reference Citations?

Reference citations in the text of your paper serve several functions. The most obvious, perhaps, is that they give credit for words, data, or even general ideas to the individual who originally presented them — it's a way of giving credit where it's due. But perhaps because of this, student writers sometimes avoid using citations. They often have the misconception that if they cite the work of others throughout their writing, it will appear as if they cannot (or are not) thinking for themselves — that they are not doing their share of work. Actually, comprehensive citation of the works of others often demonstrates the *strength* of your scholarship — it shows that you have successfully familiarized yourself with the literature in your area. In fact, failing to include major references on your subject is a sign of inadequate work on your part.

Another function of reference citations is that they permit interested readers to go to other sources which may expand upon points the writer is making. As we've said in earlier chapters, this is an important technique that you, as a researcher, should use when gathering information.

Finally, reference citations also serve to protect the writer from appearing to make unsubstantiated claims. By citing appropriate sources you are informing the reader that other credible sources (assuming that you are using credible publications) support your argument. By citing a conclusion or interpretation of findings, you are informing the reader that the conclusion has been judged to have some merit by professionals in the field. Thus, reference citations add substance to your argument. (As we noted in Chapter 6, however, some sources are more credible than others; you should keep these distinctions in mind when gathering and integrating information.)

When Should You Use Reference Citations?

Whenever you use or refer to the data, words, or even general ideas of others, you must identify the source(s) in the text of your paper. Including the reference in your bibliography is not enough because this does not allow the reader to determine precisely which ideas or words should be credited to the other individual(s). Check your school's policy on what constitutes plagiarism.

Sometimes you may have arrived at a particular idea yourself and, then, through further reading, you'll find another author who makes the same point. By all means, cite the reference. It won't detract from your contribution; instead, as we said above, your ability to document a point with a published work will (1) add strength to your argument, (2) demonstrate your familiarity with the work in the field, and (3) allow the reader to read someone else's discussion of the point if they wish.

How Do You Present Reference Citations?

APA citation style is fairly easy to learn. The author's last name and the year of publication are noted in the text. Typically you will enclose the entire citation in parentheses, like this:

```
A recent survey of adolescents (Loh, 1986) revealed
that. . . .
```

Be certain to place the citation at a point in your sentence or paragraph which clearly identifies the portion of the narrative to which the citation refers. Consider the different implications of the following two examples:

> While research on physical attractiveness has shown important developmental changes (York, 1986), these findings may be artifacts of the experimental designs.

> While research on physical attractiveness has shown important developmental changes, these findings may be artifacts of the experimental designs (York, 1986).

The second example indicates that York (1986) argued that the developmental changes may be artifacts of experimental design. In the first example, York (1986) is credited only with demonstrating developmental changes associated with physical attractiveness.

You may incorporate the author's name and/or the date in the text. In that case they should be omitted from the parenthetical information:

> In her survey of adolescents, Loh (1986) found that. . . .

> A 1986 survey of adolescents (Loh) revealed. . . .

> Based on a 1986 survey, Loh reported that. . . .

Quotations

Include the page number(s) from which the quotation was taken immediately following the author's surname and the publication date:

> She stated, "The Berster-Rand hypothesis is totally unsupported by recent research" (Carson, 1986, p. 309).

Or, cite page numbers at the end of the quotation, like this:

> Carson (1986) argued that "the Berster-Rand hypothesis is totally unsupported by recent research" (p. 309).

If you are quoting a passage of more than forty words, start the quotation on a new line, do not use quotation marks, and *block* it by indenting the entire passage five spaces from the left margin. Citations at the end of a block quote should be placed after the final punctuation mark.

> In her most recent statement of her position, Carson (1986) argued the following:
>
> > The Berster-Rand hypothesis is totally unsupported by recent research. If psychologists were to examine the experimental procedures more closely rather than focus on the outcomes alone, they would recognize that many of the findings thought to support the Berster-Rand hypothesis are, in fact, addressing very different questions (pp. 309–310).

Repeated Citation of a Source Within a Paragraph

When repeating a particular citation within any given paragraph, you needn't repeat the publication date as long as the source would not be confused with another source in the paper. However, if in doubt, repeat the full citation — its purpose is to provide clarity for the reader.

> Brown (1982) argued that aggression can only be defined relative to the context in which the behavior is expressed. Whereas Whitman (1972) had suggested that aggression should be judged irrespective of the situation, Brown contended that to do so would lead to meaningless analyses.

A Work by Two Authors

Cite both names each time the reference occurs. When the authors' names are a part of the narrative, join the names with "and"; when the authors' names are in parentheses, join the names with an ampersand (&).

> Teti and Gibbs (1985) found that infant/sibling interaction varies as a function of the age-spacing between the children.

```
Infant/sibling interaction appears to vary as a
function of the age-spacing between the children
(Teti & Gibbs, 1985).
```

A Work by More than Two and Fewer than Six Authors

Cite all names in the reference the first time you cite the source; subsequently, use only the surname of the first author, followed by "et al.":

`(Johnson, George, Evan, & Munroe, 1984)` [*first citation*]

`(Johnson et al., 1984)` [*subsequent citations*]

A Work by Six or More Authors

Cite the surname of the first author followed by "et al." in the first as well as in subsequent citations:

```
A major analysis (Brockner et al., 1985)
found. . . .
```

A Work by an Institutional Author

Authorship of a work is sometimes attributed to a government agency, a society, or some other institution. In this case, the institution is cited as the author:

```
In the final report (National Institutes of Health,
1980). . . .
```

Common abbreviations may be used or an abbreviation established in the first citation to be used subsequently, provided the meaning is clear:

`(UNICEF, 1986)` [*common abbreviation*]

`(Society for Research in Child Development [SRCD], 1982)` [*first citation*]

`(SRCD, 1982)` [*subsequent citations*]

A Work With No Author Given

When a book or article appears without an author's name, use the title instead. (Pamphlets, magazine and newspaper articles, and even books may lack a byline.) Titles of periodicals and books should be underlined; titles of articles or chapters should be enclosed in double quotation marks:

```
(Webster's New Collegiate Dictionary, 1980)

It has been argued ("Tips for preventing stress,"
1981) that. . . .
```

Citing a Work Discussed in a Secondary Source

You should always read the original source when possible. However, you may read an article which discusses material from another source that is unavailable to you; perhaps it refers to an unpublished paper or even a journal that you are unable to locate. In this instance, be certain to cite the original source with the secondary source you are using:

```
Mason's unpublished study (as cited in Mar-Chun,
1979) suggested. . . .

Gordon (1941, as cited by Howell, 1985)
discussed. . . .
```

By making it clear that your information was gained from a secondary source, you are not only giving credit to the author(s) who interpreted the material for you, but you are also protecting yourself from criticism that you misinterpreted the original source. According to APA format, you should include only the secondary source (Mar-Chun, 1979) in your reference list. However, many professors prefer that you include the primary source as well, so ask your instructor.

Authors with the Same Surname

If your paper includes citations to two authors with the same surname, include the author's initials whenever *either* is cited, to avoid confusion:

```
J.M. Schwaber (1984) studied. . . .

Further research (S.E. Schwaber, 1986) found. . . .
```

Two or More Works Within the Same Parentheses

Works by the same author(s) are arranged in order of publication from the earliest to the most recent:

```
Additional research (Whipple & Brent, 1979, 1983)
found. . . .
```

Works by different authors are arranged alphabetically by surnames:

```
Several studies have reached the same conclusions
(Livingston & Livingston, 1980; Watts, 1979, 1984;
Zen et al., 1986).
```

Two or More Works by the Same Author and Published in the Same Year

If two or more citations refer to work by the same author(s) published in the same year, label each "a," "b," and so on (through the alphabet), placing the letter immediately after the publication date. Use the same notations throughout your text citations and in your reference list.

```
Field work on parakeets (LeGault, 1985a, 1985b)
revealed. . . .

Whereas one study (LeGault, 1985a) demonstrated
. . . another (LeGault, 1985b) indicated
that. . . .
```

Personal Communication
[*letters, interviews, phone conversations*]

```
Geraldine Ferraro (personal communication, May 15,
1983) emphasized that. . . .
```

Personal communications are not included in the list of references because they cannot be consulted by the reader.

FOOTNOTES

Footnotes or endnotes are rarely used in psychology. Include a note only if you must add essential information that supplements, but cannot be integrated into, the text. Notes should be numbered consecutively throughout the paper. Type raised arabic numerals to call attention to a note (e.g., like this[1]). Type all notes on a separate sheet headed "Footnotes"; insert this sheet after your reference list, but before any tables, figures, and appendixes.

REFERENCES

A list of your references belongs at the end of your paper or article. It should include every reference you have cited in the paper, but no others. Therefore, unless your professor tells you otherwise, you should *omit* those sources which you read but did not specifically cite in your paper. Although each part of a paper should be done with great care, compiling the list of references calls for exacting precision. A misspelled name, an incorrect page number, an omitted date — any of these interferes with the reader's ability to locate the source, and calls into question the accuracy of the research and the researcher.

Before we present specific examples of references, here are a few general guidelines for composing reference lists:

1. The list of references begins on a separate page immediately following the text of the paper (that is, preceding any tables, figures, or appendixes you might include). The word "References" is centered at the top of the page.

2. The entries are listed alphabetically by the authors' last names or, in the case of institutional authorship, by the first significant word of the name (for example, The Xerox Corporation would be listed under X).

   a. If several sources have precisely the same author(s), order the entries by publication date from the earliest to the latest.
   b. Entries with the same first author but different second authors should be alphabetized by the second authors' surnames.
   c. If different entries are authored by individuals with the same surname, alphabetize them according to the authors' first initials.

```
Watts, D. N. (1976). Masking. . . .
Watts, D. N. (1986). Control of. . . .
Watts, D. N., & Brooks, B. B. (1981). Father and
   son. . . .
Watts, D. N., & Tucker, B. W. (1985). Infant. . . .
Watts, E. R. (1983). Sibling. . . .
```

3. Use hanging indentation: The first line of each entry begins at the left margin; subsequent lines are indented three spaces.

4. Capitalize only the first word of the title and the subtitle of books and articles.

5. Use "pp." to indicate page numbers in books, magazines, and newspapers, but not to refer to journal articles.

References to Periodicals

Journal Article by One Author

Include, in sequence, the author's last name, first and middle initials, publication date (in parentheses), title of the article, title of the periodical (underlined), volume of the periodical (underlined), and pages of the article.

Schacter, D. L. (1986). Amnesia and crime: How much do we really know? American Psychologist, 3, 286–295.

Include the issue number of the journal in parentheses immediately after the volume number, for example *3*(2), only if each issue is renumbered from page 1.

Journal Article by Two Authors

Bouton, M. E., & King, D. A. (1986). Effect of context on performance to conditioned stimuli with mixed histories of reinforcement and nonreinforcement. Journal of Experimental Psychology: Animal Behavior Processes, 1, 4–15.

Journal Article by More than Two Authors

McKenry, P. C., Hamdorf, K. G., Walters, C. M., & Murray, C. I. Family and job influences on role satisfaction of employed rural mothers. Psychology of Women Quarterly, 9, 242–257.

Journal Article in Press

Compas, B. E., Wagner, B. M., Slavin, L. A., & Vannatta, K. (in press). A prospective study of life events, social support and psychological symptomatology during the transition from high school to college. American Journal of Community Psychology.

Magazine Article With Discontinuous Pages

Steinem, G. (1984, October). The Ferraro factor: What difference can one woman make? Ms., pp. 43–49, 146–147.

(When an article of any kind appears on discontinuous pages, include all the page numbers with a comma between the discontinuous pages.)

Newspaper Article

Stewart, S. A. (1985, December 11). Temperament, not poor training, ignites tantrums. USA Today, p. 7D.

Newspaper Article With No Author

Insurer worried about tax status. (1986, March 28). The Burlington Free Press, p. 6B.

Entire Issue of a Journal

VandenBos, G. R. (Ed.). (1986). Psychotherapy research [Special issue]. American Psychologist, 41 (2).

Monograph

Slaughter, D. T. (1983). Early intervention and its effects on maternal and child development. Monographs of the Society for Research in Child Development. 48(4, Serial No. 202).

Immediately following the volume, in parentheses, are the issue and serial numbers. Some monographs use a *whole* number instead of a serial number; if so, indicate that number instead, for example: *17*(2, Whole No. 41).

Periodical Published Annually

Marshall, J. F. (1984). Brain function: Neural adaptations and recovery from injury. Annual Review of Psychology, 35, 277–308.

Review of a Book

Healy, C. C. (1984). Systems as targets and contexts for counseling psychology [Review of Counseling psychology in community settings]. Contemporary Psychology, 29, 236.

If the review itself had not been titled, the reference would have been:

Healy, C. C. (1984). Review of Counseling psychology in community settings. Contemporary Psychology, 29, 236.

References to Books

Book by One Author

Include, in sequence, the author's last name, first and middle initials, publication date (in parentheses), title of the book (underlined), edition if other than the first (in parentheses), city of publication, state of publication abbreviated with U.S. postal codes (include only if the city cannot be easily identified) and name of publisher, excluding terms like *Publishers* and *Inc.*, which are not important for identification.

Horowitz, M. J. (1978). Image formation and cognition (2d ed.). New York: Appleton-Century-Crofts.

Book by Two or More Authors

Lumsden, C. J., & Wilson, E. O. (1981). Genes, mind, and culture: The coevolutionary process. Cambridge, MA: Harvard University Press.

Book by an Institutional Author, Third Edition, Published by Author

American Psychological Association. (1983). Publication manual of the American Psychological Association (3rd. ed.). Washington, DC: Author.

Book Without an Author or Editor

SPSSx: User's guide. (1983). Chicago: SPSS.

Edited Book

Sigel, I. E. (Ed.). (1985). Parental belief systems: The psychological consequences for children. Hillsdale, NJ: Lawrence Erlbaum.

Note the *Ed.* refers to *editor,* whereas *ed.* refers to *edition.*

Chapter in an Edited Book

Danish, S. J., Galambos, N. L., & Laquatra, I. (1983). Life development intervention: Skill training for personal competence. In R. D. Felner, L. A. Jason, J. N. Moritsugu, & S. S. Farber (Eds.). Preventive psychology (pp. 49–61). New York: Pergamon.

Note that when the editor's name is not in the author position, you do not invert the name and initials. Also note that the page numbers of the chapter are included.

Chapter in an Edited Book that is Part of a Multivolume Work, Each Volume Having Its Own Title

Ansbacher, H. L. (1978). What is positive mental health? In D. G. Forgays (Ed.). Primary Prevention of Psychopathology: Vol. 2. Environmental influences (pp. 3–6). Hanover, NH: University Press of New England.

Published Report

Silverman, P. R. (1978). Mutual help groups and the role of the mental health professional (NIMH, DHEW Publication No. ADM 78-646). Washington, DC: U.S. Government Printing Office.

References to Unpublished Sources

Unpublished Manuscript

Dawson, B., de Armas, A., McGrath, M., & Kelly, J. A. (1985). Cognitive problem-solving training to improve the child-care judgement of child neglectful parents. Unpublished manuscript, University of Mississippi Medical Center.

Unpublished Paper Presented at a Meeting

Johnson, J. E., Yu, S., & Roopnarine, J. (1980, March). Social cognitive ability, interpersonal behaviors, and peer status within a mixed age group. Paper presented at the meeting of the Southwestern Society for Research in Human Development, Lawrence, KS.

MATCHING REFERENCES TO CITATIONS

Because accurate and comprehensive citations and references are so critical to a paper, you should take extra care to check and recheck them. As you read through your final draft, place a check next to each source in your reference list as it is cited. At the same time: (a) note and correct any inconsistencies in the spelling or order of authors' names; (b) note and correct any inconsistencies in the publication dates; and (c) be certain all the sources you have cited are included in the reference list and that you have not referenced any sources which are not cited in the text. These inconsistencies often result from deletions or additions of citations made during the revision process, so be certain to recheck your reference list *after* you have completed the final draft of your paper.

[10] A Concise Guide to Usage

PREVIEW: *In this chapter we present ten rules or principles of effective writing, chosen because they cause so much trouble for unwary writers. Read through the chapter to familiarize yourself with the material, then refer to it again as you revise and proofread your work.*

The rules are covered in the following order:

1. *Subject and verb must agree in number.*
2. *A pronoun must agree in number with its antecedent.*
3. *Use the correct form of the pronoun.*
4. *Don't shift verb tenses unnecessarily.*
5. *Place modifiers as close as possible to words modified.*
6. *Write complete sentences.*
7. *Avoid comma splice and run-on.*
8. *Distinguish between homophones.*
9. *Avoid gender-biased language.*
10. *Avoid ethnic-biased language.*

USAGE is the name given to matters of correctness or suitability of language — simple as that. Most of us learn standard usage from parents, friends, teachers, newspapers and books, radio and television. But we all have distracting lapses and weak points in our writing. That is the reason for this section of the *Writer's Guide*. The rules explained below cover the most common questions of usage. Mastering them will help you to write more clearly and without the distractions that errors of usage can cause your reader.

Rule 1. Subject and Verb Must Agree in Number

In English, nouns (and pronouns) and verbs are either singular or plural. If the subject noun (or pronoun) is singular, then the verb of the sentence must also be singular.

[**singular subject**]	[**singular verb**]
Ellen (She)	swims.
[**plural subject**]	[**plural verb**]
The girls (They)	swim.

So far, so good. But sentences like these aren't the ones that give writers problems. The difficulty surfaces when you write a sentence like this one:

> The definition of learning according to the two theories differ greatly.

Does that look all right to you? Let's see: The subject is *definition,* singular; the verb is *differ,* plural. Subject and verb do not agree. This kind of error is common, especially in speaking. You hear the noun nearest to the verb, *theories,* and create a plural verb to match. Of course, *theories* is not the subject; *definition* is. The correct sentence reads:

> The definition of learning according to the two theories differs greatly.

A simple test for complicated sentences is to omit everything but subject and verb, then look and listen:

> The definition . . . differs. . . .

Collective nouns name a group or collection: *herd, club, nation, team,* etc. They take a singular verb if unity is stressed or a plural verb if their plurality is emphasized:

> "The faculty *is* empowered to revise the curriculum."
>
> but
>
> "The faculty *are* divided on the issue of union representation."

Rule 2. A Pronoun Must Agree in Number With Its Antecedent

If the antecedent (the noun that the pronoun replaces) is singular, the pronoun must be singular. If the antecedent is plural, the pronoun must be plural:

> Many people [**plural antecedent**] fail to file their [**plural pronoun**] income taxes on time.

This would seem an easy rule to follow, yet mistakes are common. One student's explanation of how to teach windsurfing contained this sentence: "Let the learner practice until they feel quite comfortable." Here the subject ("learner") is singular, but the pronoun ("they") is plural. One way of correcting this sentence is to make the noun plural: "Let learners practice until they feel quite comfortable." This solution avoids the problem of gender introduced by the alternative: "Let the learner practice until he (she? he or she?) feels quite comfortable."

Rule 3. Use the Correct Form of the Pronoun

The common personal pronouns (*I, me, he, him, she, her, it, we, us, you, they, them*) seldom cause much difficulty. Many writers do have problems with the punctuation of two classes of possessive pronouns. **The apostrophe is never used with these forms:**

possessive forms (act as modifiers)		**substantive forms** (act as nouns)	
my	*my* pen	mine	That pen is *mine.*
your	*your* books	yours	Which books are *yours?*
his	*his* belt	his	The brown belt is *his.*
her	*her* car	hers	The car is *hers.*
its	*its* clarity	its	Of the wines tested for clarity, *its* is best.
our	*our* house	ours	The yellow house is *ours.*
your	*your* camera	yours	What kind of camera is *yours?*
their	*their* papers	theirs	The papers on the desk are *theirs.*

Note: it's is a contraction of *it is.*

Rule 4. Don't Shift Verb Tenses Unnecessarily

Traditionally, writers in some fields use only the past tense of verbs, treating all events and ideas as if they occurred in the past. Writers in other fields may sometimes use the historical present, treating past events as if they were happening now: "Shakespeare frequently alternates scenes of terror and tragedy with moments of comic relief." Use whichever tense best suits your needs. Just be consistent: Don't shift from past to present to past without a purpose.

Rule 5. Place Modifiers as Close as Possible to Words Modified

Writers-in-training are more apt to violate this rule with multi-word modifiers:

> Mangy and flea-bitten, I saw the dog sitting on my front steps.
>
> Our agency rents cars to salespeople of all sizes.
>
> Bouncing off parked cars, he spotted the driverless truck.

The meaning is clarified by placing the modifiers next to the words described:

> I saw the mangy and flea-bitten dog sitting on my front steps.
>
> Our agency rents cars of all sizes to salespeople.
>
> He spotted the driverless truck bouncing off parked cars.

Rule 6. Write Complete Sentences

A **sentence** is a group of words that contains a subject and a verb and expresses a complete thought. This is a sentence:

> My shoe is tight.

This is not:

> Because my shoe is tight.

Why not? What's the difference? Each group of words has a subject, *shoe*, and a verb, *is*. The only difference between the utterances is the addition of the word *because* to the second. The reason that "Because my shoe is tight" is not a sentence is that it doesn't express a complete thought; it cannot function as an independent unit.

Read it aloud and you'll see what we mean. The listener (reader) is left dangling — because my shoe is tight *what?**

Ironically, by adding a word, *because,* to the sentence, we've made it less than complete. This kind of word is called a **subordinator.** One kind of subordinator is the **relative pronoun:** *which, that, who, whom, what,* and *whose* are examples. The **subordinating conjunction** is a second kind. Common subordinating conjunctions are *because, after, when, although, as, before, if, unless, until, where.* The effect of adding these subordinators to a clause is to make that clause dependent.

"Because my shoe is tight" is an example of one kind of sentence fragment. It doesn't express a complete thought; it cannot stand alone. It must be attached to a complete sentence, like this:

My foot hurts because my shoe is tight.

The sentence above has two **clauses.** Because the first clause, *my foot hurts,* expresses a complete thought and can stand alone, it is called **independent.** Because the second clause does not express a complete thought and cannot stand alone, it is called **dependent.**

A complete sentence, then, must contain an independent clause. It may contain additional elements as well.

complete sentence	(*independent clause*): Stan stopped smoking recently.
complete sentence	(*two independent clauses and coordinating conjunction*): Stan stopped smoking recently, and he feels healthier.
complete sentence	(*dependent clause and independent clause*): Since Stan stopped smoking recently, he feels healthier.

Rule 7. Avoid Comma Splice and Run-On

When independent clauses are joined, you must separate them with a comma plus *and, but, or, for, nor,* or *yet;* or with a colon; or with

*Speech and writing have different requirements. In the following conversation, "because my shoe is tight" may function perfectly well: "Why are you limping?" "Because my shoe is tight."

a semicolon. Violations of this rule are the comma splice and the run-on sentence.

incorrect	The fluorescent light over the desk in my office isn't working, it hasn't worked since the painters were here. (*comma splice*)
correct	The fluorescent light over the desk in my office isn't working, and it hasn't worked since the painters were here.
correct	The fluorescent light over the desk in my office isn't working; it hasn't worked since the painters were here.

Note: See Chapter 11 for use of the colon.

Rule 8. Distinguish Between Homophones

Homophones are words pronounced alike but different in spelling and meaning. Using any of them incorrectly marks your writing as less than meticulous. You should master these common ones:

1. *their, there, they're*

   their is a possessive pronoun:

   on their own, their books

   there has three common uses:

   - as an adverb meaning *in, at,* or *to that place:*

     She is going to build an addition there.

   - as a noun meaning *that place*:

     We live near there.

   - as a function word to introduce a clause:

     There are only two choices in the matter.

   they're is a contraction of *they are:*

   They're my best friends.

2. *to, too, two*

to is a preposition meaning *toward, as far as, until,* etc. With a verb, it is a sign of the infinitive:

The road to Jeffersonville is closed.

The second shift is from three to eleven.

The plant manager likes to play squash. (**infinitive**)

too is an adverb meaning *also, more than enough:*

The report was late too.

Too many cooks spoil the broth.

two is the number between one and three, used as an adjective or a pronoun:

"Two hamburgers, please." (**adjective**)

Only two survived. (**pronoun**)

3. *than, then*

than is a conjunction used in comparison:

She is taller than her brother.

then may be an adverb, adjective, or noun related to time:

I'm going to the meeting too. I'll see you then.

Since then he hasn't smiled.

Rule 9. Avoid Gender-Biased Language

In recent years we have become much more aware of the ways language shapes our thinking. You may feel you are conscious of avoiding stereotyping in your writing, but gender-biased language has been so much a part of our lives that it is easy to overlook. Consider this statement:

Many great scholars have also managed to maintain active lives at home, remaining involved with their wives and children.

What's wrong with that sentence? What's wrong is the assumption that great scholars are all men. That is simply not true. It is this kind of bias, perhaps unconscious, perhaps unintentional, that you should avoid in your writing.

Avoiding sexist language isn't always easy. Because the English language lacks a singular pronoun that means *he or she,* the writer constantly has to deal with gender choices like these:

> When the shopper wishes to cash a check, he (she?). . . .
>
> Each student should write her (or his?) name at the top.

As a writer, you do have options:

1. Alternate female and male pronouns:

    > Each student should write his name at the top. If a student would like to take the exam early, she should speak with the professor.

2. Rewrite to use the plural:

    > Students should write their names at the top. If students would like to take the exam early, they should speak with the professor.

3. Rewrite to avoid gender pronouns:

    > The student's name should be written at the top. A student who wishes to take the exam early should speak with the professor.

Sometimes it seems difficult to avoid sexist language because a number of English terms are gender-biased themselves: *chairman, mailman, policeman,* and so on. However, with just a little thought, alternative terms are available: *chairperson, mail carrier, police officer.*

The *Publication Manual of the American Psychological Association* (1983) presents detailed guidelines for using nonsexist language. Take a look.

Rule 10. Avoid Ethnic-Biased Language

Most people realize that referring to Italians as "wops" not only demeans Italians but also promotes inaccurate stereotypes. Such an obvious form of stereotyping may seem easy for you to detect and avoid. But other ethnic-biased language is more subtle and common.

For example, a term such as "culturally deprived" is frequently used to refer to any group that lives in poverty, despite the fact that the group may enjoy an extremely rich cultural heritage and ongoing tradition. Their culture may be different from the writer's, but this is certainly insufficient to conclude that culture is lacking.

As a general guide in all your writing:

1. choose terms that are **specific** rather than general (for example, *low income, lacking formal education*);
2. choose terms which are **nonevaluative,** unless you have actual data to support the evaluation.

[11] *Make Punctuation Work for You*

PREVIEW: *Correctly used, punctuation aids the reader's understanding of your writing. Incorrectly used, punctuation can confuse or misinform. This chapter focuses on the most common uses of each mark of punctuation. Read through the chapter to familiarize yourself with the material, then refer to it again as you revise and proofread your work.*

Punctuation marks are covered in the following order:

Comma
Semicolon
Colon
Apostrophe
Parentheses
Brackets
Ellipsis
Dash
Quotation Marks

We use punctuation marks to clarify the meaning of our writing. Some usages are purely conventional, the colon (:) after "Dear Sir" in a business letter, for instance. Others have been established to make meaning clear. Your primary goal in punctuating should always be clarity of expression.

The sections in this book which discuss documentation, research proposals and reports, and literature reviews note conventions in punctuation which are particular to psychology. In contrast, this chapter will note more general guidelines for using punctuation in all of the writing you do. Although common sense will often help you select the correct usage, there is no substitute for knowing a few basic rules.

Comma ,

The comma is the most frequently used, and abused, mark of punctuation. Relatively weak as a separator, it is less emphatic than the colon, semicolon, or dash. It indicates the briefest of pauses. Although there are dozens of uses of the comma, we'll look at only the most common.

To separate items in a series:

> The standard personal computer consists of memory, video display, keyboard, disc drive, and printer.

Note: a comma is used before the *and.*

To set off interrupters:

> The party's candidate for governor, Marie Marshall, offered her plan to reduce the deficit. (**appositive**)
>
> The flight from Chicago, on the other hand, arrived on time. (**parenthetical expression**)

Note: Interrupters are enclosed by a *pair* of commas.

To set off a long introductory phrase or clause:

> In the deep snows at the top of the mountain, they hid a cache of supplies.
>
> If you want to learn to ski the right way, you should take lessons.

To separate independent clauses joined by and, but, or, nor, for, yet:

> Matt was interested in the job, but he didn't want to move away from his family.
>
> The purchasing department ordered new furniture, and the office manager had the rooms painted.

To introduce a short quotation:

> The librarian told them, "If you have a question, ask someone."

Semicolon ;

The semicolon provides more separation than the comma, less than the period. Its most common use is to separate independent clauses not joined by *and, but, or, nor, for, yet,* when you wish to show close relationship between those clauses. Otherwise, use a period.

> The dean wanted a new curriculum; the faculty did not.
>
> My mother was understanding the first time; she was upset the second time; the third time she was furious.

TO REVIEW: To show the degree of relationship between independent clauses, you have three options: semicolon, period, and comma with coordinating conjunction (*and, but, or, nor, for, yet*):

> The legislature has been meeting since January; they have not passed a single bill.
>
> The legislature has been meeting since January. They have not passed a single bill.
>
> The legislature has been meeting since January, yet they have not passed a single bill.

Colon :

The colon is used primarily to introduce a word, phrase, or clause that fulfills or explains an idea in the first part of the sentence. It is also used after the salutation of a business letter, to introduce a list, and to separate the title and subtitle of a book. Because it is a strong mark of punctuation, use only as directed.

To introduce or fulfill:

> In that respect, Canada is like the United States: Both have large numbers of non-English speakers.
>
> On his deathbed the old miser made only one request: that his gold be buried with him.

To introduce a list:

> The demographic study focused on three factors: population, income, and age.

Note: Do not use a colon directly after a verb.

Incorrect	On her trip to France she visited: Paris, Chartres, and Mont St. Michel.
Correct	On her trip to France she visited Paris, Chartres, and Mont St. Michel.

After the salutation of a business letter:

Dear Ms. Irving:

To separate the title and the subtitle of a book:

The Golden Bough: A Study in Magic and Religion

Apostrophe ’

The apostrophe has three distinct uses: to mark the omission of one or more letters or numerals, to mark the possessive case, and to mark certain plurals.

To mark the omission of a letter or letters:

wouldn’t	(would not)
can’t	(cannot)
you’ll	(you will)
I’m	(I am)
it’s	(it is)
they’re	(they are)

To mark the omission of one or more numerals:

a ’57 Chevy	a 1957 Chevy
the summer of ’42	the summer of 1942

To form the possessive of a singular or plural noun not ending in s:

girl	girl’s
laboratory	laboratory’s
men	men’s
children	children’s

To form the possessive of a plural noun ending in s:

girls	girls'
books	books'
laboratories	laboratories'

To form the possessive of a singular noun of one syllable ending in s *or* s *sound:*

William James	William James's philosophy
Brahms	Brahms's First Symphony

To form the possessive of a singular noun of more than one syllable ending in s *or* s *sound:*

Socrates	Socrates' school

Note: Do not use an apostrophe with possessive pronouns: *his, hers, yours, ours, theirs, whose, its* (*it's* means *it is*).

Parentheses ( )

Parentheses are used to enclose explanatory material within a sentence when such material is incidental to the main thought. Commas may also be used for this purpose; they are less formal and indicate a closer relationship to the main sentence than parentheses. Some writers use parentheses for the same purpose.

> Senator Mason (who just happens to be my sister-in-law) wrote the new farm credit bill.
>
> Of his many novels (he wrote more than thirty), *Stairway to Darkness* was his favorite.

Note: Parentheses are sometimes used in other ways in citations and references. See the section on documentation.

Brackets [ ]

Brackets are marks of punctuation with limited but specific uses, especially in academic writing. Often when you excerpt part of a longer quotation, the meaning is not entirely clear. You may add clarification in brackets.

> "The President [Kennedy] was determined that mental health become a national priority."
>
> "Freud's division of the psyche [id, ego, superego] has been disputed by many in recent years."

When you wish to acknowledge without changing an error in the quoted material, enclose the Latin word *sic* (thus) in brackets:

> The client wrote that his "childrun [sic] can't learn."

Note: Many typewriters do not have brackets. You can ink them in by hand. Do *not* use parentheses instead of brackets.

Ellipsis . . .

The omission (ellipsis) of part of a quoted passage is indicated by ellipsis marks: three spaced periods. Use these marks when you are quoting a long passage but wish to omit material.

> "These matriarchal tribes . . . introduced new values to the existing order."

When you delete the end of a sentence, use four periods:

> "Four score and seven years ago our fathers brought forth on this continent, a new nation. . . . Now we are engaged in a great civil war, testing whether that nation, or any nation so conceived and so dedicated, can long endure."

Dash —

The dash is probably the most overused mark of punctuation. Because it is so emphatic, its misuse stands out glaringly and is viewed as the sign of an overemotional style. Employ the dash only as described below.

To show an abrupt break in thought:

> "I explained all that to you yesterday when — oh, but that wasn't you."

To introduce a word or words for emphasis:

> You have only one choice — do it!

To separate a final summarizing clause from the preceding idea:

> Food, clothing, shelter, and fuel — these are all that Thoreau claimed are needed to sustain life.

Note: To type a dash, use two hyphens (--). Do not leave a space before or after the hyphens.

Quotation Marks " "

Quotation marks enclose the precise words spoken or written by someone other than the writer. Do not use them to identify indirect quotations or summaries.

To enclose direct quotations:

> In her book, Conway asserts that "imitation does not necessarily imply identification."
>
> Piaget's statement, "To understand is to invent," has great implications for education.

EXCEPTION: Long quotations (more than forty words) are indented five spaces and double spaced. Quotation marks are not used. See section on documentation (Chapter 9, p. 189).

A quotation within a quotation uses **single marks within double marks:**

> In her opening statements she urged her listeners to "recall our leader's warning that 'only mutual respect will promote a healthy society.'"

Note: Periods and commas are placed inside the quotation marks. Semicolons and colons are placed outside. Question marks, exclamation points, and dashes are placed outside the quotation marks unless they are part of the original quotation.

To mark the titles of short stories, poems, essays, articles, and chapters of books, songs, symphonies, and plays in a collection:

Hemingway's story "The Snows of Kilimanjaro"

Shelley's poem "To a Skylark"

Note: Titles of books, full-length plays, magazines, and newspapers are *italicized* or *underlined,* not placed in quotation marks.

References

American Psychological Association. (1983). *Publication manual of the American Psychological Association* (3rd ed.). Washington, DC: Author.

Barzun, J. (1971). *On writing, editing, and publishing.* Chicago: University of Chicago Press.

Berthoff, A. (1978). *Forming, thinking, writing: The composing imagination.* Rochelle Park, NJ: Hayden.

Cohen, S., & Wills, T. A. (1985). Stress, social support, and the buffering hypothesis. *Psychological Bulletin, 98,* 310–357.

Foucault, M. (1970). *The order of things* (M. Foucault, Trans.). New York: Pantheon Books. (Original work published 1966).

Freedman, J. L. (1984). Effect of television violence on aggressiveness. *Psychological Bulletin, 96,* 227–246.

Friere, P. (1970). *Pedagogy of the oppressed.* New York: Herder & Herder.

Kilmer, S. (1979). Infant-toddler group day care: A review of research. In L. G. Katz (Ed.), *Current topics in early childhood education* (pp. 69–115). Norwood, NJ: Ablex.

Light, R. J., & Pillemer, D. B. (1984). *Summing up: The science of reviewing research.* Cambridge, MA: Harvard University Press.

Rosenthal, R., & Rubin, D. B. (1982). Further meta-analytic procedures for assessing cognitive gender differences. *Journal of Educational Psychology, 74,* 708–712.

Sternberg, R. J. (1977). *Writing the psychology paper.* Woodbury, NY: Barron's Educational Series.

Strachey, J. (1955). *The standard edition of the complete psychological works of Sigmund Freud. Vol. XVIII: Beyond the pleasure principle, group psychology, and other works.* London: Hogarth Press.

Thorpe, G. L. (1984). Operant learning in physical rehabilitation [Review of *Behavioral approaches to rehabilitation: Coping with change*]. *Contemporary Psychology, 29,* 906.

Index

2 3 4 5 6 7 8 9 0